Clojure High Performance Programming

Second Edition

Become an expert at writing fast and high performant code in Clojure 1.7.0

Shantanu Kumar

[PACKT] open source✺
PUBLISHING   community experience distilled

BIRMINGHAM - MUMBAI

Clojure High Performance Programming
Second Edition

First published: November 2013

Second edition: September 2015

Production reference: 1230915

Published by Packt Publishing Ltd.
Livery Place
35 Livery Street
Birmingham B3 2PB, UK.

ISBN 978-1-78528-364-2

www.packtpub.com

Credits

Author

Shantanu Kumar

Reviewers

Eduard Bondarenko

Matjaz Gregoric

Commissioning Editor

Nadeem Bagban

Acquisition Editor

Larissa Pinto

Content Development Editor

Divij Kotian

Technical Editor

Anushree Arun Tendulkar

Copy Editor

Yesha Gangani

Project Coordinator

Nikhil Nair

Proofreader

Safis Editing

Indexer

Tejal Soni

Graphics

Abhinash Sahu

Production Coordinator

Manu Joseph

Cover Work

Manu Joseph

About the Author

Shantanu Kumar is a software developer living in Bengaluru, India. He works with Concur Technologies as a principal engineer, building a next-generation stack in Clojure. He started learning computer programming when he was at school, and has dabbled in several programming languages and software technologies. Having used Java for a long time, he discovered Clojure in early 2009 and has been a fan of it ever since.

When not busy with programming or reading up on technical stuff, he enjoys reading non-fiction and cycling around Bengaluru. Shantanu is an active participant in The Bangalore Clojure Users Group, and contributes to several open source Clojure projects on GitHub. He is also the author of the first edition of the book *Clojure High Performance Programming, Packt Publishing*.

I am grateful to my colleagues, Saju Pillai and Vijay Mathew, at Concur India for imparting marathon performance analysis/tuning sessions. I appreciate the input received from Andy Fingerhut and Zach Tellman on certain topics during the course of writing the second edition of the book. I also want to thank the technical reviewers and the team at Packt for their valuable input and support.

Writing this book has been an arduous task. I want to thank my family for putting up with me while I was immersed in this book for far too many days and weekends. If not for their support, I would not have been able to do justice to the book.

About the Reviewers

Eduard Bondarenko is a software developer living in Kiev, Ukraine. He started programming using Basic on ZXSpectrum a long time ago. Later, he worked professionally in the web development domain.

Eduard used Ruby on Rails for many years. Having used Ruby for a long time, he discovered Clojure in early 2009 and liked the language. Besides Ruby and Clojure, he is also interested in Erlang, Scala languages, machine learning, and logic programming.

Matjaz Gregoric is a software developer living in Ljubljana, Slovenia, with his wife and two children. He has a BS degree in physics, and has been developing software professionally since 2007.

During his career, Matjaz worked on various projects where he was able to get familiar with different technologies and programming languages. In 2010, he got familiar with Clojure and immediately fell in love with it. He is currently working on scalable distributed systems and complex web UIs.

ww.PacktPub.com

Support files, eBooks, discount offers, and more

For support files and downloads related to your book, please visit www.PacktPub.com.

Did you know that Packt offers eBook versions of every book published, with PDF and ePub files available? You can upgrade to the eBook version at www.PacktPub.com and as a print book customer, you are entitled to a discount on the eBook copy. Get in touch with us at service@packtpub.com for more details.

At www.PacktPub.com, you can also read a collection of free technical articles, sign up for a range of free newsletters and receive exclusive discounts and offers on Packt books and eBooks.

https://www2.packtpub.com/books/subscription/packtlib

Do you need instant solutions to your IT questions? PacktLib is Packt's online digital book library. Here, you can search, access, and read Packt's entire library of books.

Why subscribe?

- Fully searchable across every book published by Packt
- Copy and paste, print, and bookmark content
- On demand and accessible via a web browser

Free access for Packt account holders

If you have an account with Packt at www.PacktPub.com, you can use this to access PacktLib today and view 9 entirely free books. Simply use your login credentials for immediate access.

Table of Contents

Preface

Since the first edition of this book was published in November 2013, Clojure has seen a much wider adoption and has witnessed many success stories. The newer versions of Clojure fortify its performance story while staying close to its roots—simplicity and pragmatism. This edition significantly updates the book for Clojure 1.7, and adds a new chapter on the performance measurement.

The Java Virtual Machine plays a huge role in the performance of the Clojure programs. This edition of the book increases the focus on the JVM tools for performance management, and it explores how to use those. This book is updated to use Java 8, though it also highlights the places where features from Java 7 or 8 have been used.

This book is updated mainly to be more of practical use to the readers. I hope that this edition will better equip the readers with performance measurement and profiling tools and with the know-how of analyzing and tuning the performance characteristics of Clojure code.

What this book covers

Chapter 1, *Performance by Design*, classifies the various use cases with respect to performance, and analyzes how to interpret their performance aspects and needs.

Chapter 2, *Clojure Abstractions*, is a guided tour of various Clojure data structures, abstractions (persistent data structures, vars, macros, transducers, and so on), and their performance characteristics.

Chapter 3, *Leaning on Java*, discusses how to enhance performance by using Java interoperability and features from Clojure.

Chapter 4, *Host Performance*, discusses how the host stack impacts performance. Being a hosted language, Clojure has its performance directly related to the host.

Chapter 5, *Concurrency*, is an advanced chapter that discusses the concurrency and parallelism features in Clojure and JVM. Concurrency is an increasingly significant way to derive performance.

Chapter 6, *Measuring Performance*, covers various aspects of performance benchmarks and measuring other factors.

Chapter 7, *Performance Optimization*, discusses systematic steps that need to be taken in order to identify that the performance bottlenecks obtain good performance.

Chapter 8, *Application Performance*, discusses building applications for performance. This involves dealing with external subsystems and factors that impact the overall performance.

What you need for this book

You should acquire Java Development Kit version 8 or higher for your operating system to work through all the examples. This book discusses the Oracle HotSpot JVM, so you may want to get Oracle JDK or OpenJDK (or Zulu) if possible. You should also get the latest Leiningen version (2.5.2 as of the time of writing) from `http://leiningen.org/`, and JD-GUI from `http://jd.benow.ca/`.

Who this book is for

This book is for intermediate Clojure programmers who are interested in learning how to write high-performance code. If you are an absolute beginner in Clojure, you should learn the basics of the language first, and then come back to this book. You need not be well-versed in performance engineering or Java. However, some prior knowledge of Java would make it much easier to understand the Java-related chapters.

Conventions

In this book, you will find a number of text styles that distinguish between different kinds of information. Here are some examples of these styles and an explanation of their meaning.

Code words in text, database table names, folder names, filenames, file extensions, pathnames, dummy URLs, user input, and Twitter handles are shown as follows: "Note that `identical?` in Clojure is the same as `==` in Java."

A block of code is set as follows:

```
user=> (identical? "foo" "foo")  ; literals are automatically interned
true
user=> (identical? (String. "foo") (String. "foo"))  ; created string
is not interned
false
```

New terms and **important words** are shown in bold. Words that you see on the screen, for example, in menus or dialog boxes, appear in the text like this: "Clicking the **Next** button moves you to the next screen."

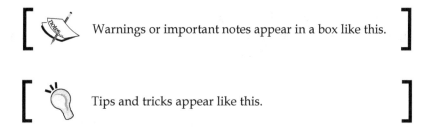

Warnings or important notes appear in a box like this.

Tips and tricks appear like this.

Reader feedback

Feedback from our readers is always welcome. Let us know what you think about this book — what you liked or disliked. Reader feedback is important for us as it helps us develop titles that you will really get the most out of.

To send us general feedback, simply e-mail feedback@packtpub.com, and mention the book's title in the subject of your message.

If there is a topic that you have expertise in and you are interested in either writing or contributing to a book, see our author guide at www.packtpub.com/authors.

Customer support

Now that you are the proud owner of a Packt book, we have a number of things to help you to get the most from your purchase.

Errata

Although we have taken every care to ensure the accuracy of our content, mistakes do happen. If you find a mistake in one of our books—maybe a mistake in the text or the code—we would be grateful if you could report this to us. By doing so, you can save other readers from frustration and help us improve subsequent versions of this book. If you find any errata, please report them by visiting `http://www.packtpub.com/submit-errata`, selecting your book, clicking on the **Errata Submission Form** link, and entering the details of your errata. Once your errata are verified, your submission will be accepted and the errata will be uploaded to our website or added to any list of existing errata under the Errata section of that title.

To view the previously submitted errata, go to `https://www.packtpub.com/books/content/support` and enter the name of the book in the search field. The required information will appear under the **Errata** section.

Piracy

Piracy of copyrighted material on the Internet is an ongoing problem across all media. At Packt, we take the protection of our copyright and licenses very seriously. If you come across any illegal copies of our works in any form on the Internet, please provide us with the location address or website name immediately so that we can pursue a remedy.

Please contact us at `copyright@packtpub.com` with a link to the suspected pirated material.

We appreciate your help in protecting our authors and our ability to bring you valuable content.

eBooks, discount offers, and more

Did you know that Packt offers eBook versions of every book published, with PDF and ePub files available? You can upgrade to the eBook version at `www.PacktPub.com` and as a print book customer, you are entitled to a discount on the eBook copy. Get in touch with us at `customercare@packtpub.com` for more details.

At `www.PacktPub.com`, you can also read a collection of free technical articles, sign up for a range of free newsletters, and receive exclusive discounts and offers on Packt books and eBooks.

Questions

If you have a problem with any aspect of this book, you can contact us at
questions@packtpub.com, and we will do our best to address the problem.

Performance by Design

Clojure is a safe, functional programming language that brings great power and simplicity to the user. Clojure is also dynamically and strongly typed, and has very good performance characteristics. Naturally, every activity performed on a computer has an associated cost. What constitutes acceptable performance varies from one use-case and workload to another. In today's world, performance is even the determining factor for several kinds of applications. We will discuss Clojure (which runs on the **JVM (Java Virtual Machine)**), and its runtime environment in the light of performance, which is the goal of this book.

The performance of Clojure applications depend on various factors. For a given application, understanding its use cases, design and implementation, algorithms, resource requirements and alignment with the hardware, and the underlying software capabilities is essential. In this chapter, we will study the basics of performance analysis, including the following:

- Classifying the performance anticipations by the use cases types
- Outlining the structured approach to analyze performance
- A glossary of terms, commonly used to discuss performance aspects
- The performance numbers that every programmer should know

Use case classification

The performance requirements and priority vary across the different kinds of use cases. We need to determine what constitutes acceptable performance for the various kinds of use cases. Hence, we classify them to identify their performance model. When it comes to details, there is no sure shot performance recipe for any kind of use case, but it certainly helps to study their general nature. Note that in real life, the use cases listed in this section may overlap with each other.

The user-facing software

The performance of user-facing applications is strongly linked to the user's anticipation. Having a difference of a good number of milliseconds may not be perceptible for the user but at the same time, a wait of more than a few seconds may not be taken kindly. One important element in normalizing anticipation is to engage the user by providing duration-based feedback. A good idea to deal with such a scenario would be to start the task asynchronously in the background, and poll it from the UI layer to generate a duration-based feedback for the user. Another way could be to incrementally render the results to the user to even out the anticipation.

Anticipation is not the only factor in user facing performance. Common techniques like staging or precomputation of data, and other general optimization techniques can go a long way to improve the user experience with respect to performance. Bear in mind that all kinds of user facing interfaces fall into this use case category — the Web, mobile web, GUI, command line, touch, voice-operated, gesture...you name it.

Computational and data-processing tasks

Non-trivial compute intensive tasks demand a proportional amount of computational resources. All of the CPU, cache, memory, efficiency and the parallelizability of the computation algorithms would be involved in determining the performance. When the computation is combined with distribution over a network or reading from/staging to disk, I/O bound factors come into play. This class of workloads can be further subclassified into more specific use cases.

A CPU bound computation

A CPU bound computation is limited by the CPU cycles spent on executing it. Arithmetic processing in a loop, small matrix multiplication, determining whether a number is a **Mersenne prime**, and so on, would be considered CPU bound jobs. If the algorithm complexity is linked to the number of iterations/operations N, such as $O(N)$, $O(N^2)$ and more, then the performance depends on how big N is, and how many CPU cycles each step takes. For parallelizable algorithms, performance of such tasks may be enhanced by assigning multiple CPU cores to the task. On virtual hardware, the performance may be impacted if the CPU cycles are available in bursts.

A memory bound task

A memory bound task is limited by the availability and bandwidth of the memory. Examples include large text processing, list processing, and more. For example, specifically in Clojure, the (reduce f (pmap g coll)) operation would be memory bound if coll is a large sequence of big maps, even though we parallelize the operation using pmap here. Note that higher CPU resources cannot help when memory is the bottleneck, and vice versa. Lack of availability of memory may force you to process smaller chunks of data at a time, even if you have enough CPU resources at your disposal. If the maximum speed of your memory is X and your algorithm on single the core accesses the memory at speed $X/3$, the multicore performance of your algorithm cannot exceed three times the current performance, no matter how many CPU cores you assign to it. The memory architecture (for example, SMP and NUMA) contributes to the memory bandwidth in multicore computers. Performance with respect to memory is also subject to page faults.

A cache bound task

A task is cache bound when its speed is constrained by the amount of cache available. When a task retrieves values from a small number of repeated memory locations, for example a small matrix multiplication, the values may be cached and fetched from there. Note that CPUs (typically) have multiple layers of cache, and the performance will be at its best when the processed data fits in the cache, but the processing will still happen, more slowly, when the data does not fit into the cache. It is possible to make the most of the cache using **cache-oblivious** algorithms. A higher number of concurrent cache/memory bound threads than CPU cores is likely to flush the instruction pipeline, as well as the cache at the time of context switch, likely leading to a severely degraded performance.

An input/output bound task

An **input/output (I/O)** bound task would go faster if the I/O subsystem, that it depends on, goes faster. Disk/storage and network are the most commonly used I/O subsystems in data processing, but it can be serial port, a USB-connected card reader, or any I/O device. An I/O bound task may consume very few CPU cycles. Depending on the speed of the device, connection pooling, data compression, asynchronous handling, application caching, and more, may help in performance. One notable aspect of I/O bound tasks is that performance is usually dependent on the time spent waiting for connection/seek, and the amount of serialization that we do, and hardly on the other resources.

In practice, many data processing workloads are usually a combination of CPU bound, memory bound, cache bound, and I/O bound tasks. The performance of such mixed workloads effectively depends on the even distribution of CPU, cache, memory, and I/O resources over the duration of the operation. A bottleneck situation arises only when one resource gets too busy to make way for another.

Online transaction processing

Online transaction processing (OLTP) systems process the business transactions on demand. They can sit behind systems such as a user-facing ATM machine, point-of-sale terminal, a network-connected ticket counter, ERP systems, and more. The OLTP systems are characterized by low latency, availability, and data integrity. They run day-to-day business transactions. Any interruption or outage is likely to have a direct and immediate impact on sales or service. Such systems are expected to be designed for resiliency rather than delayed recovery from failures. When the performance objective is unspecified, you may like to consider graceful degradation as a strategy.

It is a common mistake to ask the OLTP systems to answer analytical queries, something that they are not optimized for. It is desirable for an informed programmer to know the capability of the system, and suggest design changes as per the requirements.

Online analytical processing

Online analytical processing (OLAP) systems are designed to answer analytical queries in a short time. They typically get data from the OLTP operations, and their data model is optimized for querying. They basically provide for consolidation (roll-up), drill-down and slicing and dicing of data for analytical purposes. They often use specialized data stores that can optimize ad-hoc analytical queries on the fly. It is important for such databases to provide pivot-table like capability. Often, the OLAP cube is used to get fast access to the analytical data.

Feeding the OLTP data into the OLAP systems may entail workflows and multistage batch processing. The performance concern of such systems is to efficiently deal with large quantities of data while also dealing with inevitable failures and recovery.

Batch processing

Batch processing is automated execution of predefined jobs. These are typically bulk jobs that are executed during off-peak hours. Batch processing may involve one or more stages of job processing. Often batch processing is clubbed with workflow automation, where some workflow steps are executed offline. Many of the batch processing jobs work on staging of data, and on preparing data for the next stage of processing to pick up.

Batch jobs are generally optimized for the best utilization of the computing resources. Since there is little to moderate the demand to lower the latencies of some particular subtasks, these systems tend to optimize for throughput. A lot of batch jobs involve largely I/O processing and are often distributed over a cluster. Due to distribution, the data locality is preferred when processing the jobs; that is, the data and processing should be local in order to avoid network latency in reading/writing data.

A structured approach to the performance

In practice, the performance of non-trivial applications is rarely a function of coincidence or prediction. For many projects, performance is not an option (it is rather a necessity), which is why this is even more important today. Capacity planning, determining performance objectives, performance modeling, measurement, and monitoring are key.

Tuning a poorly designed system to perform is significantly harder, if not practically impossible, than having a system well-designed from the start. In order to meet a performance goal, performance objectives should be known before the application is designed. The performance objectives are stated in terms of latency, throughput, resource utilization, and workload. These terms are discussed in the following section in this chapter.

The resource cost can be identified in terms of application scenarios, such as browsing of products, adding products to shopping cart, checkout, and more. Creating workload profiles that represent users performing various operations is usually helpful.

Performance modeling is a reality check for whether the application design will support the performance objectives. It includes performance objectives, application scenarios, constraints, measurements (benchmark results), workload objectives and if available, the performance baseline. It is not a replacement for measurement and load testing, rather, the model is validated using these. The performance model may include the performance test cases to assert the performance characteristics of the application scenarios.

Deploying an application to production almost always needs some form of **capacity planning**. It has to take into account the performance objectives for today and for the foreseeable future. It requires an idea of the application architecture, and an understanding of how the external factors translate into the internal workload. It also requires informed expectations about the responsiveness and the level of service to be provided by the system. Often, capacity planning is done early in a project to mitigate the risk of provisioning delays.

The performance vocabulary

There are several technical terms that are heavily used in performance engineering. It is important to understand these, as they form the cornerstone of the performance-related discussions. Collectively, these terms form a performance vocabulary. The performance is usually measured in terms of several parameters, where every parameter has roles to play—such parameters are a part of the vocabulary.

Latency

Latency is the time taken by an individual unit of work to complete the task. It does not imply successful completion of a task. Latency is not collective, it is linked to a particular task. If two similar jobs—`j1` and `j2` took 3 ms and 5 ms respectively, their latencies would be treated as such. If `j1` and `j2` were dissimilar tasks, it would have made no difference. In many cases the average latency of similar jobs is used in the performance objectives, measurement, and monitoring results.

Latency is an important indicator of the health of a system. A high performance system often thrives on low latency. Higher than normal latency can be caused due to load or bottleneck. It helps to measure the latency distribution during a load test. For example, if more than 25 percent of similar jobs, under a similar load, have significantly higher latency than others, then it may be an indicator of a bottleneck scenario that is worth investigating.

When a task called j1 consists of smaller tasks called j2, j3, and j4, the latency of j1 is not necessarily the sum of the latencies of each of j2, j3, and j4. If any of the subtasks of j1 are concurrent with another, the latency of j1 will turn out to be less than the sum of the latencies of j2, j3, and j4. The I/O bound tasks are generally more prone to higher latency. In network systems, latency is commonly based on the round-trip to another host, including the latency from source to destination, and then back to source.

Throughput

Throughput is the number of successful tasks or operations performed in a unit of time. The top-level operations performed in a unit of time are usually of a similar kind, but with a potentially different from latencies. So, what does throughput tell us about the system? It is the rate at which the system is performing. When you perform load testing, you can determine the maximum rate at which a particular system can perform. However, this is not a guarantee of the conclusive, overall, and maximum rate of performance.

Throughput is one of the factors that determine the scalability of a system. The throughput of a higher level task depends on the capacity to spawn multiple such tasks in parallel, and also on the average latency of those tasks. The throughput should be measured during load testing and performance monitoring to determine the peak-measured throughput, and the maximum-sustained throughput. These factors contribute to the scale and performance of a system.

Bandwidth

Bandwidth is the raw data rate over a communication channel, measured in a certain number of bits per second. This includes not only the payload, but also all the overhead necessary to carry out the communication. Some examples are: Kbits/sec, Mbits/sec, and more. An uppercase B such as KB/sec denotes Bytes, as in kilobytes per second. Bandwidth is often compared to throughput. While bandwidth is the raw capacity, throughput for the same system is the successful task completion rate, which usually involves a round-trip. Note that throughput is for an operation that involves latency. To achieve maximum throughput for a given bandwidth, the communication/protocol overhead and operational latency should be minimal.

For storage systems (such as hard disks, solid-state drives, and more) the predominant way to measure performance is **IOPS (Input-output per second)**, which is multiplied by the transfer size and represented as bytes per second, or further into MB/sec, GB/sec, and more. IOPS is usually derived for sequential and random workloads for read/write operations.

Mapping the throughput of a system to the bandwidth of another may lead to dealing with an impedance mismatch between the two. For example, an order processing system may perform the following tasks:

- Transact with the database on disk

- Post results over the network to an external system

Depending on the bandwidth of the disk sub-system, the bandwidth of the network, and the execution model of order processing, the throughput may depend not only on the bandwidth of the disk sub-system and network, but also on how loaded they currently are. Parallelism and pipelining are common ways to increase the throughput over a given bandwidth.

Baseline and benchmark

The performance **baseline**, or simply baseline, is the reference point, including measurements of well-characterized and understood performance parameters for a known configuration. The baseline is used to collect performance measurements for the same parameters that we may benchmark later for another configuration. For example, collecting "throughput distribution over 10 minutes at a load of 50 concurrent threads" is one such performance parameter that we can use for baseline and benchmarking. A baseline is recorded together with the hardware, network, OS and JVM configuration.

The performance **benchmark**, or simply benchmark, is the recording of the performance parameter measurements under various test conditions. A benchmark can be composed of a performance test suite. A benchmark may collect small to large amounts of data, and may take varying durations depending on the use-cases, scenarios, and environment characteristics.

A baseline is a result of the benchmark that was conducted at one point in time. However, a benchmark is independent of the baseline.

Profiling

Performance profiling, or simply profiling, is the analysis of the execution of a program at its runtime. A program can perform poorly for a variety of reasons. A **profiler** can analyze and find out the execution time of various parts of the program. It is possible to put statements in a program manually to print the execution time of the blocks of code, but it gets very cumbersome as you try to refine the code iteratively.

A profiler is of great assistance to the developer. Going by how profilers work, there are three major kinds—instrumenting, sampling, and event-based.

- **Event-based profilers**: These profilers work only for selected language platforms, and provide a good balance between the overhead and results; Java supports event-based profiling via the JVMTI interface.

- **The instrumenting profilers**: These profilers modify code at either compile time, or runtime to inject performance counters. They are intrusive by nature and add significant performance overhead. However, you can profile the regions of code very selectively using the instrumenting profilers.

- **The sampling profilers**: These profilers pause the runtime and collect its state at "sampling intervals". By collecting enough samples, they get to know where the program is spending most of its time. For example, at a sampling interval of 1 millisecond, the profiler would have collected 1000 samples in a second. A sampling profiler also works for code that executes faster than the sampling interval (as in, the code may perform several iterations of work between the two sampling events), as the frequency of pausing and sampling is proportional to the overall execution time of any code.

Profiling is not meant only for measuring execution time. Capable profilers can provide a view of memory analysis, garbage collection, threads, and more. A combination of such tools is helpful to find memory leaks, garbage collection issues, and so on.

Performance optimization

Simply put, **optimization** is enhancing a program's resource consumption after a performance analysis. The symptoms of a poorly performing program are observed in terms of high latency, low throughput, unresponsiveness, instability, high memory consumption, high CPU consumption, and more. During the performance analysis, one may profile the program in order to identify the bottlenecks and tune the performance incrementally by observing the performance parameters.

Better and suitable algorithms are an all-around good way to optimize code. The CPU bound code can be optimized with computationally cheaper operations. The cache bound code can try using less memory lookups to keep a good hit ratio. The memory bound code can use an adaptive memory usage and conservative data representation to store in memory for optimization. The I/O bound code can attempt to serialize as little data as possible, and batching of operations will make the operation less chatty for better performance. Parallelism and distribution are other, overall good ways to increase performance.

Concurrency and parallelism

Most of the computer hardware and operating systems that we use today provide concurrency. On the x86 architecture, hardware support for concurrency can be traced as far back as the 80286 chip. **Concurrency** is the simultaneous execution of more than one process on the same computer. In older processors, concurrency was implemented using the context switch by the operating system kernel. When concurrent parts are executed in parallel by the hardware instead of merely the switching context, it is called **parallelism**. Parallelism is the property of the hardware, though the software stack must support it in order for you to leverage it in your programs. We must write your program in a concurrent way to exploit the parallelism features of the hardware.

While concurrency is a natural way to exploit hardware parallelism and speed up operations, it is worth bearing in mind that having significantly higher concurrency than the parallelism that your hardware can support is likely to schedule tasks to varying processor cores thereby, lowering the branch prediction and increasing cache misses.

At a low level, spawning the processes/threads, mutexes, semaphores, locking, shared memory, and interprocess communication are used for concurrency. The JVM has an excellent support for these concurrency primitives and interthread communication. Clojure has both—the low and higher level concurrency primitives that we will discuss in the concurrency chapter.

Resource utilization

Resource utilization is the measure of the server, network, and storage resources that is consumed by an application. Resources include CPU, memory, disk I/O, network I/O, and more. The application can be analyzed in terms of CPU bound, memory bound, cache bound, and I/O bound tasks. Resource utilization can be derived by means of benchmarking, by measuring the utilization at a given throughput.

Workload

Workload is the quantification of how much work is there in hand to be carried out by the application. It is measured in the total numbers of users, the concurrent active users, the transaction volume, the data volume, and more. Processing a workload should take in to account the load conditions, such as how much data the database currently holds, how filled up the message queues are, the backlog of I/O tasks after which the new load will be processed, and more.

The latency numbers that every programmer should know

Hardware and software have progressed over the years. Latencies for various operations put things in perspective. The latency numbers for the year 2015, reproduced with the permission of Aurojit Panda and Colin Scott of Berkeley University (`http://www.eecs.berkeley.edu/~rcs/research/interactive_latency.html`). Latency numbers that every programmer should know are as shown in the following table:

Operation	Time taken as of 2015
L1 cache reference	1ns (nano second)
Branch mispredict	3 ns
L2 cache reference	4 ns
Mutex lock/unlock	17 ns
Compress 1KB with Zippy (Zippy/Snappy: `http://code.google.com/p/snappy/`)	2µs (1000 ns = 1µs: micro second)
Send 2000 bytes over the commodity network	200ns (that is, 0.2µs)
SSD random read	16 µs
Round-trip in the same datacenter	500 µs
Read 1,000,000 bytes sequentially from SSD	200 µs
Disk seek	4 ms (1000 µs = 1 ms)
Read 1,000,000 bytes sequentially from disk	2 ms
Packet roundtrip CA to Netherlands	150 ms

The preceding table shows the operations in a computer vis-a-vis the latency incurred due to the operation. When a CPU core processes some data in a CPU register, it may take a few CPU cycles (for reference, a 3 GHz CPU runs 3000 cycles per nanosecond), but the moment it has to fall back on L1 or L2 cache, the latency becomes thousands of times slower. The preceding table does not show main memory access latency, which is roughly 100 ns (it varies, based on the access pattern) — about 25 times slower than the L2 cache.

Summary

We learned about the basics of what it is like to think more deeply about performance. We saw the common performance vocabulary, and also the use cases by which performance aspects might vary. We concluded by looking at the performance numbers for the different hardware components, which is how performance benefits reach our applications. In the next chapter, we will dive into the performance aspects of the various Clojure abstractions.

2
Clojure Abstractions

Clojure has four founding ideas. Firstly, it was set up to be a functional language. It is not pure (as in purely functional), but emphasizes immutability. Secondly, it is a dialect of Lisp; Clojure is malleable enough that users can extend the language without waiting for the language implementers to add new features and constructs. Thirdly, it was built to leverage concurrency for the new generation challenges. Lastly, it was designed to be a hosted language. As of today, Clojure implementations exist for the JVM, CLR, JavaScript, Python, Ruby, and Scheme. Clojure blends seamlessly with its host language.

Clojure is rich in abstractions. Though the syntax itself is very minimal, the abstractions are finely grained, mostly composable, and designed to tackle a wide variety of concerns in the least complicated way. In this chapter, we will discuss the following topics:

- Performance characteristics of non-numeric scalars
- Immutability and epochal time model paving the way for performance by isolation
- Persistent data structures and their performance characteristics
- Laziness and its impact on performance
- Transients as a high-performance, short-term escape hatch
- Other abstractions, such as tail recursion, protocols/types, multimethods, and many more

Non-numeric scalars and interning

Strings and characters in Clojure are the same as in Java. The string literals are implicitly interned. Interning is a way of storing only the unique values in the heap and sharing the reference everywhere it is required. Depending on the JVM vendor and the version of Java you use, the interned data may be stored in a string pool, Permgen, ordinary heap, or some special area in the heap marked for interned data. Interned data is subject to garbage collection when not in use, just like ordinary objects. Take a look at the following code:

```
user=> (identical? "foo" "foo")   ; literals are automatically interned
true
user=> (identical? (String. "foo") (String. "foo"))   ; created string
is not interned
false
user=> (identical? (.intern (String. "foo")) (.intern (String.
"foo")))
true
user=> (identical? (str "f" "oo") (str "f" "oo"))   ; str creates
string
false
user=> (identical? (str "foo") (str "foo"))   ; str does not create
string for 1 arg
true
user=> (identical? (read-string "\"foo\"") (read-string "\"foo\""))   ;
not interned
false
user=> (require '[clojure.edn :as edn])   ; introduced in Clojure 1.5
nil
user=> (identical? (edn/read-string "\"foo\"") (edn/read-string
"\"foo\""))
false
```

Note that `identical?` in Clojure is the same as `==` in Java. The benefit of interning a string is that there is no memory allocation overhead for duplicate strings. Commonly, applications on the JVM spend quite some time on string processing. So, it makes sense to have them interned whenever there is a chance of duplicate strings being simultaneously processed. Most of the JVM implementations today have an extremely fast intern operation; however, you should measure the overhead for your JVM if you have an older version.

Another benefit of string interning is that when you know that two string tokens are interned, you can compare them faster for equality using `identical?` than non-interned string tokens. The equivalence function `=` first checks for identical references before conducting a content check.

Symbols in Clojure always contain interned string references within them, so generating a symbol from a given string is nearly as fast as interning a string. However, two symbols created from the same string will not be identical:

```
user=> (identical? (.intern "foo") (.intern "foo"))
true
user=> (identical? (symbol "foo") (symbol "foo"))
false
user=> (identical? (symbol (.intern "foo")) (symbol (.intern "foo")))
false
```

Keywords are, on the basis of their implementation, built on top of symbols and are designed to work with the `identical?` function for equivalence. So, comparing keywords for equality using `identical?` would be faster, just as with interned string tokens.

Clojure is increasingly being used for large-volume data processing, which includes text and composite data structures. In many cases, the data is either stored as JSON or EDN (`http://edn-format.org`). When processing such data, you can save memory by interning strings or using symbols/keywords. Remember that string tokens read from such data would not be automatically interned, whereas the symbols and keywords read from EDN data would invariably be interned. You may come across such situations when dealing with relational or NoSQL databases, web services, CSV or XML files, log parsing, and so on.

Interning is linked to the JVM **Garbage Collection** (**GC**), which, in turn, is closely linked to performance. When you do not intern the string data and let duplicates exist, they end up being allocated on the heap. More heap usage leads to GC overhead. Interning a string has a tiny but measurable and upfront performance overhead, whereas GC is often unpredictable and unclear. GC performance, in most JVM implementations, has not increased in a similar proportion to the performance advances in hardware. So, often, effective performance depends on preventing GC from becoming the bottleneck, which in most cases means minimizing it.

Identity, value, and epochal time model

One of the principal virtues of Clojure is its simple design that results in malleable, beautiful composability. Using symbols in place of pointers is a programming practice that has existed for several decades now. It has found widespread adoption in several imperative languages. Clojure dissects that notion in order to uncover the core concerns that need to be addressed. The following subsections illustrate this aspect of Clojure.

We program using logical entities to represent values. For example, a value of 30 means nothing unless it is associated with a logical entity, let's say age. The logical entity age is the identity here. Now, even though age represents a value, the value may change with time; this brings us to the notion of state, which represents the value of the identity at a certain time. Hence, state is a function of time and is causally related to what we do in the program. Clojure's power lies in binding an identity with its value that holds true at the time and the identity remains isolated from any new value it may represent later. We will discuss state management in *Chapter 5, Concurrency*.

Variables and mutation

If you have previously worked with an imperative language (C/C++, Java, and so on), you may be familiar with the concept of a variable. A **variable** is a reference to a block of memory. When we update its value, we essentially update the place in memory where the value is stored. The variable continues to point to the place where the older version of the value was stored. So, essentially, a variable is an alias for the place of storage of values.

A little analysis would reveal that variables are strongly linked to the processes that read or mutate their values. Every mutation is a state transition. The processes that read/update the variable should be aware of the possible states of the variable to make sense of the state. Can you see a problem here? It conflates identity and state! It is impossible to refer to a value or a state in time when dealing with a variable — the value could change at any time unless you have complete control over the process accessing it. The mutability model does not accommodate the concept of time that causes its state transition.

The issues with mutability do not stop here. When you have a composite data structure containing mutable variables, the entire data structure becomes mutable. How can we mutate it without potentially undermining the other processes that might be observing it? How can we share this data structure with concurrent processes? How can we use this data structure as a key in a hash-map? This data structure does not convey anything. Its meaning could change with mutation! How do we send such a thing to another process without also compensating for the time, which can mutate it in different ways?

Immutability is an important tenet of functional programming. It not only simplifies the programming model, but also paves the way for safety and concurrency. Clojure supports immutability throughout the language. Clojure also supports fast, mutation-oriented data structures as well as thread-safe state management via concurrency primitives. We will discuss these topics in the forthcoming sections and chapters.

Collection types

There are a few types of collections in Clojure, which are categorized based on their properties. The following Venn diagram depicts this categorization on the basis of whether the collections are counted (so that `counted?` returns `true`) or associative (so that `associative?` returns `true`) or sequential (so that `sequential?` returns `true`):

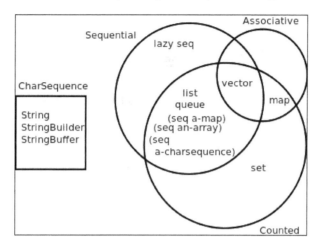

The previous diagram illustrates the characteristics that different kinds of data structures share. The sequential structures let us iterate over the items in the collection, the item count of counted structures can be found constant with respect to time, and associative structures can be looked at with keys for corresponding values. The **CharSequence** box shows the character sequence Java types that can be converted to a Clojure sequence using (`seq charseq`).

Persistent data structures

As we've noticed in the previous section, Clojure's data structures are not only immutable, but can produce new values without impacting the old version. Operations produce these new values in such a way that old values remain accessible; the new version is produced in compliance with the complexity guarantees of that data structure, and both the old and new versions continue to meet the complexity guarantees. The operations can be recursively applied and can still meet the complexity guarantees. Such immutable data structures as the ones provided by Clojure are called **persistent data structures**. They are "persistent", as in, when a new version is created, both the old and new versions "persist" in terms of both the value and complexity guarantee. They have nothing to do with storage or durability of data. Making changes to the old version doesn't impede working with the new version and vice versa. Both versions persist in a similar way.

Among the publications that have inspired the implementation of Clojure's persistent data structures, two of them are well known. Chris Okasaki's *Purely Functional Data Structures* has influenced the implementation of persistent data structures and lazy sequences/operations. Clojure's persistent queue implementation is adapted from Okasaki's *Batched Queues*. Phil Bagwell's *Ideal Hash Tries*, though meant for mutable and imperative data structures, was adapted to implement Clojure's persistent map/vector/set.

Constructing lesser-used data structures

Clojure supports a well-known literal syntax for lists, vectors, sets, and maps. Shown in the following list are some less-used methods for creating other data structures:

- Map (`PersistentArrayMap` and `PersistentHashMap`):

  ```
  {:a 10 :b 20}  ; array-map up to 8 pairs
  {:a 1 :b 2 :c 3 :d 4 :e 5 :f 6 :g 7 :h 8 :i 9}  ; hash-map for 9
  or more pairs
  ```

- Sorted map (`PersistentTreeMap`):

  ```
  (sorted-map :a 10 :b 20 :c 30)  ; (keys ..) should return sorted
  ```

- Sorted set (`PersistentTreeSet`):

  ```
  (sorted-set :a :b :c)
  ```

- Queue (`PersistentQueue`):

  ```
  (import 'clojure.lang.PersistentQueue)
  (reduce conj PersistentQueue/EMPTY [:a :b :c :d])  ; add to queue
  (peek queue)  ; read from queue
  (pop queue)  ; remove from queue
  ```

As you can see, abstractions such as `TreeMap` (sorted by key), `TreeSet` (sorted by element), and `Queue` should be instantiated by calling their respective APIs.

Complexity guarantee

The following table gives a summary of the complexity guarantees (using the Big-O notation) of various kinds of persistent data structures in Clojure:

Operation	Persistent List	Persistent HashMap	Persistent ArrayMap	Persistent Vector	Persistent Queue	Persistent TreeMap
count	O(1)	O(1)	O(1)	O(1)	O(1)	O(1)

Operation	Persistent List	Persistent HashMap	Persistent ArrayMap	Persistent Vector	Persistent Queue	Persistent TreeMap
conj	O(1)			O(1)	O(1)	
first	O(1)			O(<7)	O(<7)	
rest	O(1)			O(<7)	O(<7)	
doseq	O(n)	O(n)	O(n)	O(n)	O(n)	
nth	O(n)			O(<7)	O(<7)	
last	O(n)			O(n)	O(n)	
get		O(<7)	O(1)	O(<7)	O(<7)	O(log n)
assoc		O(<7)	O(1)	O(<7)		O(log n)
dissoc		O(<7)	O(1)	O(<7)		O(log n)
peek				O(1)	O(1)	
pop				O(<7)	O(1)	

A **list** is a sequential data structure. It provides constant time access for count and for anything regarding the first element only. For example, conj adds the element to the head and guarantees *O(1)* complexity. Similarly, first and rest provide *O(1)* guarantees too. Everything else provides an *O(n)* complexity guarantee.

Persistent hash-maps and vectors use the trie data structure with a branching factor of 32 under the hood. So, even though the complexity is $O(log_{32} n)$, only 2^{32} hash codes can fit into the trie nodes. Hence, $log_{32} 2^{32}$, which turns out to be 6.4 and is less than 7, is the worst-case complexity and can be considered near-constant time. As the trie grows larger, the portion to copy gets proportionally tiny due to structure sharing. Persistent hash-set implementation is also based on hash-map; hence, the hash-sets share the characteristics of the hash-maps. In a persistent vector, the last incomplete node is placed at the tail, which is always directly accessible from the root. This makes using conj to the end a constant time operation.

Persistent tree-maps and tree-sets are basically sorted maps and sets respectively. Their implementation uses red-black trees and is generally more expensive than hash-maps and hash-sets. A persistent queue uses a persistent vector under the hood for adding new elements. Removing an element from a persistent queue takes the head off seq, which is created from the vector where new elements are added.

The complexity of an algorithm over a data structure is not an absolute measure of its performance. For example, working with hash-maps involves computing the hashCode, which is not included in the complexity guarantee. Our choice of data structures should be based on the actual use case. For example, when should we use a list instead of a vector? Probably when we need sequential or **last-in-first-out** (**LIFO**) access, or when constructing an **abstract-syntax-tree** (**AST**) for a function call.

O(<7) implies near constant time

You may know that the **Big-O** notation is used to express the upper bound (worst case) of the efficiency of any algorithm. The variable n is used to express the number of elements in the algorithm. For example, a binary search on a sorted associative collection, such as a sorted vector, is a logarithmic time, that is an $O(log_2 n)$ or simply an $O(log n)$ algorithm. Since there can be a maximum of 2^{32} (technically 2^{31} due to a signed positive integer) elements in a Java collection and $log_2 2^{32}$ is 32, the binary search can be $O(\leq32)$ in the worst case. Similarly, though operations on persistent collections are $O(log_{32} n)$, in the worst case they actually turn out to be $O(log_{32} 2^{32})$ at maximum, which is $O(<7)$. Note that this is much lower than logarithmic time and approaches near constant time. This implies not so bad performance for persistent collections even in the worst possible scenario.

The concatenation of persistent data structures

While persistent data structures have excellent performance characteristics, the concatenation of two persistent data structures has been a linear time $O(N)$ operation, except for some recent developments. The concat function, as of Clojure 1.7, still provides linear time concatenation. Experimental work on **Relaxed Radix Balanced** (**RRB**) trees is going on in the **core.rrb-vector** contrib project (`https://github.com/clojure/core.rrb-vector`), which may provide logarithmic time $O(log N)$ concatenation. Readers interested in the details should refer to the following links:

- The RRB-trees paper at `http://infoscience.epfl.ch/record/169879/files/RMTrees.pdf`

- Phil Bagwell's talk at `http://www.youtube.com/watch?v=K2NYwP90bNs`

- Tiark Rompf's talk at `http://skillsmatter.com/podcast/scala/fast-concatenation-immutable-vectors`

Sequences and laziness

"A seq is like a logical cursor."

– Rich Hickey

Sequences (commonly known as **seqs**) are a way to sequentially consume a succession of data. As with iterators, they let a user begin consuming elements from the head and proceed realizing one element after another. However, unlike iterators, sequences are immutable. Also, since sequences are only a view of the underlying data, they do not modify the storage structure of the data.

What makes sequences stand apart is they are not data structures per se; rather, they are a data abstraction over a stream of data. The data may be produced by an algorithm or a data source connected to an I/O operation. For example, the `resultset-seq` function accepts a `java.sql.ResultSet` JDBC instance as an argument and produces lazily realized rows of data as `seq`.

Clojure data structures can be turned into sequences using the `seq` function. For example, `(seq [:a :b :c :d])` returns a sequence. Calling `seq` over an empty collection returns nil.

Sequences can be consumed by the following functions:

- `first`: This returns the head of the sequence
- `rest`: This returns the remaining sequence, even if it's empty, after removing the head
- `next`: This returns the remaining sequence or nil, if it's empty, after removing the head

Laziness

Clojure is a strict (as in, the opposite of "lazy") language, which can choose to explicitly make use of laziness when required. Anybody can create a lazily evaluated sequence using the `lazy-seq` macro. Some Clojure operations over collections, such as `map`, `filter`, and more are intentionally lazy.

Laziness simply means that the value is not computed until actually required. Once the value is computed, it is cached so that any future reference to the value need not re-compute it. The caching of the value is called **memoization**. Laziness and memoization often go hand in hand.

Laziness in data structure operations

Laziness and memoization together form an extremely useful combination to keep the single-threaded performance of functional algorithms comparable to its imperative counterparts. For an example, consider the following Java code:

```java
List<String> titles = getTitles();
int goodCount = 0;
for (String each: titles) {
  String checksum = computeChecksum(each);
  if (verifyOK(checksum)) {
    goodCount++;
  }
}
```

As is clear from the preceding snippet, it has a linear time complexity, that is, $O(n)$, and the whole operation is performed in a single pass. The comparable Clojure code is as follows:

```clojure
(->> (get-titles)
  (map compute-checksum)
  (filter verify-ok?)
  count)
```

Now, since we know `map` and `filter` are lazy, we can deduce that the Clojure version also has linear time complexity, that is, $O(n)$, and finishes the task in one pass with no significant memory overhead. Imagine, for a moment, that `map` and `filter` are not lazy—what would be the complexity then? How many passes would it make? It's not just that map and filter would both have taken one pass, that is, $O(n)$, each; they would each have taken as much memory as the original collection in the worst case, due to storing the intermediate results.

It is important to know the value of laziness and memoization in an immutability-emphasizing functional language such as Clojure. They form a basis for **amortization** in persistent data structures, which is about focusing on the overall performance of a composite operation instead of microanalyzing the performance of each operation in it; the operations are tuned to perform faster in those operations that matter the most.

Another important bit of detail is that when a lazy sequence is realized, the data is memoized and stored. On the JVM, all the heap references that are reachable in some way are not garbage collected. So, as a consequence, the entire data structure is kept in the memory unless you lose the head of the sequence. When working with lazy sequences using local bindings, make sure you don't keep referring to the lazy sequence from any of the locals. When writing functions that may accept lazy sequence(s), take care that any reference to the lazy `seq` does not outlive the execution of the function in the form of a closure or some such.

Constructing lazy sequences

Now that we know what lazy sequences are, let's try to create a retry counter that should return true only as many times as the retry can be performed. This is shown in the following code:

```
(defn retry? [n]
  (if (<= n 0)
    (cons false (lazy-seq (retry? 0)))
    (cons true (lazy-seq (retry? (dec n)))))))
```

The `lazy-seq` macro makes sure that the stack is not used for recursion. We can see that this function would return endless values. Hence, in order to inspect what it returns, we should limit the number of elements as shown in the following code:

```
user=> (take 7 (retry? 5))
(true true true true true false false)
```

Now, let's try using it in a mock fashion:

```
(loop [r (retry? 5)]
  (if-not (first r)
    (println "No more retries")
    (do
      (println "Retrying")
      (recur (rest r)))))
```

As expected, the output should print `Retrying` five times before printing `No more retries` and exiting as follows:

```
Retrying
Retrying
Retrying
Retrying
Retrying
No more retries
nil
```

Let's take another simpler example of constructing a lazy sequence, which gives us a countdown from a specified number to zero:

```
(defn count-down [n]
  (if (<= n 0)
    '(0)
    (cons n (lazy-seq (count-down (dec n)))))))
```

We can inspect the values it returns as follows:

```
user=> (count-down 8)
(8 7 6 5 4 3 2 1 0)
```

Lazy sequences can loop indefinitely without exhausting the stack and can come in handy when working with other lazy operations. To maintain a balance between space-saving and performance, consuming lazy sequences results in the chunking of elements by a factor of 32. That means lazy seqs are realized in a chunk-size of 32, even though they are consumed sequentially.

Custom chunking

The default chunk size 32 may not be optimum for all lazy sequences — you can override the chunking behavior when you need to. Consider the following snippet (adapted from Kevin Downey's public gist at https://gist.github.com/hiredman/324145):

```
(defn chunked-line-seq
  "Returns the lines of text from rdr as a chunked[size] sequence of
strings.
  rdr must implement java.io.BufferedReader."
  [^java.io.BufferedReader rdr size]
  (lazy-seq
    (when-let [line (.readLine rdr)]
      (chunk-cons
        (let [buffer (chunk-buffer size)]
          (chunk-append buffer line)
          (dotimes [i (dec size)]
            (when-let [line (.readLine rdr)]
              (chunk-append buffer line)))
  (chunk buffer))
(chunked-line-seq rdr size)))))
```

As per the previous snippet, the user is allowed to pass a chunk size that is used to produce the lazy sequence. A larger chunk size may be useful when processing large text files, such as when processing CSV or log files. You would notice the following four less-known functions used in the snippet:

- clojure.core/chunk-cons
- clojure.core/chunk-buffer
- clojure.core/chunk-append
- clojure.core/chunk

While `chunk-cons` is the equivalent of `clojure.core/cons` for chunked sequences, `chunk-buffer` creates a mutable chunk buffer (controls the chunk size), `chunk-append` appends an item to the end of a mutable chunk buffer, and chunk turns a mutable chunk buffer into an immutable chunk.

The `clojure.core` namespace has several functions related to chunked sequences listed as follows:

- `chunk`
- `chunk-rest`
- `chunk-cons`
- `chunk-next`
- `chunk-first`
- `chunk-append`
- `chunked-seq?`
- `chunk-buffer`

These functions are not documented, so although I would encourage you to study their source code to understand what they do, I would advise you not to make any assumptions about their support in future Clojure versions.

Macros and closures

Often, we define a macro so as to turn the parameter body of code into a closure and delegate it to a function. See the following example:

```
(defmacro do-something
  [& body]
  `(do-something* (fn [] ~@body)))
```

When using such code, if the body binds a local to a lazy sequence it may be retained longer than necessary, likely with bad consequences on memory consumption and performance. Fortunately, this can be easily fixed:

```
(defmacro do-something
  [& body]
  `(do-something* (^:once fn* [] ~@body)))
```

Notice the `^:once` hint and the `fn*` macro, which make the Clojure compiler clear the closed-over references, thus avoiding the problem. Let's see this in action (Alan Malloy's example from `https://groups.google.com/d/msg/clojure/Ys3kEz5c_eE/3St2AbIc3zMJ`):

```
user> (let [x (for [n (range)] (make-array Object 10000))
       f (^:once fn* [] (nth x 1e6))]   ; using ^:once
         (f))
#<Object[] [Ljava.lang.Object;@402d3105>
user> (let [x (for [n (range)] (make-array Object 10000))
            f (fn* [] (nth x 1e6))]            ; not using ^:once
         (f))
OutOfMemoryError GC overhead limit exceeded
```

The manifestation of the previous condition depends on the available heap space. This issue is tricky to detect as it only raises `OutOfMemoryError`, which is easy to misunderstand as a heap space issue instead of a memory leak. As a preventive measure, I would suggest using `^:once` with `fn*` in all cases where you close over any potentially lazy sequence.

Transducers

Clojure 1.7 introduced a new abstraction called transducers for "composable algorithmic transformations", commonly used to apply a series of transformations over collections. The idea of transducers follows from the **reducing function**, which accepts arguments of the form (`result`, `input`) and returns `result`. A reducing function is what we typically use with reduce. A **transducer** accepts a reducing function, wraps/composes over its functionality to provide something extra, and returns another reducing function.

The functions in `clojure.core` that deal with collections have acquired an `arity-1` variant, which returns a transducer, namely map, cat, mapcat, filter, remove, take, take-while, take-nth, drop, drop-while, replace, partition-by, partition-all, keep, keep-indexed, dedupe and random-sample.

Consider the following few examples, all of which do the same thing:

```
user=> (reduce ((filter odd?) +) [1 2 3 4 5])
9
user=> (transduce (filter odd?) + [1 2 3 4 5])
9
user=> (defn filter-odd? [xf]
          (fn
            ([] (xf))
```

```
        ([result] (xf result))
        ([result input] (if (odd? input)
                           (xf result input)
                           result))))
#'user/filter-odd?
user=> (reduce (filter-odd? +) [1 2 3 4 5])
9
```

Here, (`filter odd?`) returns a transducer — in the first example the transducer wraps over the reducer function + to return another combined reducing function. While we use the ordinary `reduce` function in the first example, in the second example we use the `transduce` function that accepts a transducer as an argument. In the third example, we write a transducer `filter-odd?`, which emulates what (`filter odd?`) does. Let's see how the performance varies between traditional and transducer versions:

```
;; traditional way
user=> (time (dotimes [_ 10000] (reduce + (filter odd? (range
10000)))))
"Elapsed time: 2746.782033 msecs"
nil
;; using transducer
(def fodd? (filter odd?))
user=> (time (dotimes [_ 10000] (transduce fodd? + (range 10000))))
"Elapsed time: 1998.566463 msecs"
nil
```

Performance characteristics

The key point behind transducers is how orthogonal each transformation is allowed to be, yet highly composable also. At the same time, transformations can happen in lockstep for the entire sequence instead of each operation producing lazy chunked sequences. This often causes significant performance benefits with transducers. Lazy sequences are still going to be useful when the final result is too large to realize at once — for other use cases transducers should fit the need aptly with improved performance. Since the core functions have been overhauled to work with transducers, it makes sense to model transformations more often than not in terms of transducers.

Transients

Earlier in this chapter, we discussed the virtues of immutability and the pitfalls of mutability. However, even though mutability is fundamentally unsafe, it also has very good single-threaded performance. Now, what if there was a way to restrict the mutable operation in a local context in order to provide safety guarantees? That would be equivalent to combining the performance advantage and local safety guarantees. That is exactly the abstraction called **transients**, which is provided by Clojure.

Firstly, let's verify that it is safe (up to Clojure 1.6 only):

```
user=> (let [t (transient [:a])]
  @(future (conj! t :b)))
IllegalAccessError Transient used by non-owner thread  clojure.lang.
PersistentVector$TransientVector.ensureEditable (PersistentVector.
java:463)
```

As we can see previously, up to Clojure 1.6, a transient created in one thread cannot be accessed by another. However, this operation is allowed in Clojure 1.7 in order for transducers to play well with the `core.async` (https://github.com/clojure/core.async) library — the developer should maintain operational consistency on transients across threads:

```
user=> (let [t (transient [:a])] (seq t))

IllegalArgumentException Don't know how to create ISeq from: clojure.
lang.PersistentVector$TransientVector  clojure.lang.RT.seqFrom (RT.
java:505)
```

So, transients cannot be converted to seqs. Hence, they cannot participate in the birthing of new persistent data structures and leak out of the scope of execution. Consider the following code:

```
(let [t (transient [])]
  (conj! t :a)
  (persistent! t)
  (conj! t :b))
IllegalAccessError Transient used after persistent! call
clojure.lang.PersistentVector$TransientVector.ensureEditable
(PersistentVector.java:464)
```

The `persistent!` function permanently converts `transient` into an equivalent persistent data structure. Effectively, transients are for one-time use only.

Conversion between `persistent` and `transient` data structures (the `transient` and `persistent!` functions) is constant time, that is, it is an *O(1)* operation. Transients can be created from unsorted maps, vectors, and sets only. The functions that mutate transients are: `conj!`, `disj!`, `pop!`, `assoc!`, and `dissoc!`. Read-only operations such as `get`, `nth`, `count`, and many more work as usual on transients, but functions such as `contains?` and those that imply seqs, such as `first`, `rest`, and `next`, do not.

Fast repetition

The function `clojure.core/repeatedly` lets us execute a function many times and produces a lazy sequence of results. Peter Taoussanis, in his open source serialization library **Nippy** (`https://github.com/ptaoussanis/nippy`), wrote a transient-aware variant that performs significantly better. It is reproduced, as shown, with his permission (note that the arity of the function is not the same as `repeatedly`):

```
(defn repeatedly*
  "Like `repeatedly` but faster and returns given collection type."
  [coll n f]
  (if-not (instance? clojure.lang.IEditableCollection coll)
    (loop [v coll idx 0]
      (if (>= idx n)
        v
        (recur (conj v (f)) (inc idx))))
    (loop [v (transient coll) idx 0]
      (if (>= idx n)
        (persistent! v)
        (recur (conj! v (f)) (inc idx))))))
```

Performance miscellanea

Besides the major abstractions we saw earlier in the chapter, there are other smaller, but nevertheless very performance-critical, parts of Clojure that we will see in this section.

Disabling assertions in production

Assertions are very useful to catch logical errors in the code during development, but they impose a runtime overhead that you may like to avoid in the production environment. Since `assert` is a compile time variable, the assertions can be silenced either by binding `assert` to false or by using `alter-var-root` before the code is loaded. Unfortunately, both the techniques are cumbersome to use. Paul Stadig's library called **assertions** (`https://github.com/pjstadig/assertions`) helps with this exact use-case by enabling or disabling assertions via the command-line argument `-ea` to the Java runtime.

To use it, you must include it in your Leiningen `project.clj` file as a dependency:

```
:dependencies [;; other dependencies...
                          [pjstadig/assertions "0.1.0"]]
```

You must use this library's `assert` macro instead of Clojure's own, so each `ns` block in the application should look similar to this:

```
(ns example.core

  (:refer-clojure :exclude [assert])

  (:require [pjstadig.assertions :refer [assert]]))
```

When running the application, you should include the `-ea` argument to the JRE to enable assertions, whereas its exclusion implies no assertion at runtime:

```
$ JVM_OPTS=-ea lein run -m example.core
$ java -ea -jar example.jar
```

Note that this usage will not automatically avoid assertions in the dependency libraries.

Destructuring

Destructuring is one of Clojure's built-in mini languages and, arguably, a top productivity booster during development. This feature leads to the parsing of values to match the left-hand side of the binding forms. The more complicated the binding form, the more work there is that needs to be done. Not surprisingly, this has a little bit of performance overhead.

It is easy to avoid this overhead by using explicit functions to unravel data in the tight loops and other performance-critical code. After all, it all boils down to making the program work less and do more.

Recursion and tail-call optimization (TCO)

Functional languages have this concept of tail-call optimization related to recursion. So, the idea is that when a recursive call is at the tail position, it does not take up space on the stack for recursion. Clojure supports a form of user-assisted recursive call to make sure the recursive calls do not blow the stack. This is kind of an imperative looping, but is extremely fast.

When carrying out computations, it may make a lot of sense to use `loop-recur` in the tight loops instead of iterating over synthetic numbers. For example, we want to add all odd integers from zero through to 1,000,000. Let's compare the code:

```
(defn oddsum-1 [n]   ; using iteration
  (->> (range (inc n))
    (filter odd?)
    (reduce +)))
(defn oddsum-2 [n]   ; using loop-recur
  (loop [i 1 s 0]
    (if (> i n)
      s
      (recur (+ i 2) (+ s i)))))
```

When we run the code, we get interesting results:

```
user=> (time (oddsum-1 1000000))
"Elapsed time: 109.314908 msecs"

250000000000
user=> (time (oddsum-2 1000000))
"Elapsed time: 42.18116 msecs"

250000000000
```

The `time` macro is far from perfect as the performance-benchmarking tool, but the relative numbers indicate a trend — in the subsequent chapters, we will look at the *Criterium* library for more scientific benchmarking. Here, we use `loop-recur` not only to iterate faster, but we are also able to change the algorithm itself by iterating only about half as many times as we did in the other example.

Premature end of iteration

When accumulating over a collection, in some cases, we may want to end it prematurely. Prior to Clojure 1.5, `loop-recur` was the only way to do it. When using `reduce`, we can do just that using the `reduced` function introduced in Clojure 1.5 as shown:

```
;; let coll be a collection of numbers
(reduce (fn ([x] x) ([x y] (if (or (zero? x) (zero? y)) (reduced 0) (*
x y))))
            coll)
```

Here, we multiply all the numbers in a collection and, upon finding any of the numbers as zero, immediately return the result zero instead of continuing up to the last element.

The function `reduced?` helps detect when a reduced value is returned. Clojure 1.7 introduces the `ensure-reduced` function to box up non-reduced values as reduced.

Multimethods versus protocols

Multimethods are a fantastic expressive abstraction for a polymorphic dispatch on the dispatch function's return value. The `dispatch` functions associated with a multimethod are maintained at runtime and are looked up whenever a multimethod call is invoked. While multimethods provide a lot of flexibility in determining the dispatch, the performance overhead is simply too high compared to that of protocol implementations.

Protocols (`defprotocol`) are implemented using reify, records (`defrecord`), and types (`deftype`, `extend-type`) in Clojure. This is a big discussion topic—since we are discussing the performance characteristics, it should suffice to say that protocol implementations dispatch on polymorphic types and are significantly faster than multimethods. Protocols and types are generally the implementation detail of an API, so they are usually fronted by functions.

Due to the multimethods' flexibility, they still have a place. However, in performance-critical code it is advisable to use protocols, records, and types instead.

Inlining

It is well known that macros are expanded inline at the call site and avoid a function call. As a consequence, there is a small performance benefit. There is also a `definline` macro that lets you write a function just like a normal macro. It creates an actual function that gets inlined at the call site:

```
(def PI Math/PI)
(definline circumference [radius]
  `(* 2 PI ~radius))
```

 Note that the JVM also analyzes the code it runs and does its own inlining of code at runtime. While you may choose to inline the hot functions, this technique is known to give only a modest performance boost.

When we define a `var` object, its value is looked up each time it is used. When we define a `var` object using a `:const` meta pointing to a `long` or `double` value, it is inlined from wherever it is called:

```
(def ^:const PI Math/PI)
```

This is known to give a decent performance boost when applicable. See the following example:

```
user=> (def a 10)
user=> (def ^:const b 10)
user=> (def ^:dynamic c 10)
user=> (time (dotimes [_ 100000000] (inc a)))
"Elapsed time: 1023.745014 msecs"
nil
user=> (time (dotimes [_ 100000000] (inc b)))
"Elapsed time: 226.732942 msecs"
nil
user=> (time (dotimes [_ 100000000] (inc c)))
"Elapsed time: 1094.527193 msecs"
nil
```

Summary

Performance is one of the cornerstones of Clojure's design. Abstractions in Clojure are designed for simplicity, power, and safety, with performance firmly in mind. We saw the performance characteristics of various abstractions and also how to make decisions about abstractions depending on performance use cases.

In the next chapter, we will see how Clojure interoperates with Java and how we can extract Java's power to derive optimum performance.

3
Leaning on Java

Being hosted on the JVM, there are several aspects of Clojure that really help to understand about the Java language and platform. The need is not only due to interoperability with Java or understanding its implementation, but also for performance reasons. In certain cases, Clojure may not generate optimized JVM bytecode by default; in some other cases, you may want to go beyond the performance that Clojure data structures offer—you can use the Java alternatives via Clojure to get better performance. This chapter discusses those aspects of Clojure. In this chapter we will discuss:

- Inspecting Java and bytecode generated from a Clojure source
- Numerics and primitives
- Working with arrays
- Reflection and type hinting

Inspecting the equivalent Java source for Clojure code

Inspecting the equivalent Java source for a given Clojure code provides great insight into how that might impact its performance. However, Clojure generates only Java bytecodes at runtime unless we compile a namespace out to the disk. When developing with Leiningen, only selected namespaces under the `:aot` vector in the `project.clj` file are output as the compiled `.class` files containing bytecodes. Fortunately, an easy and quick way to know the equivalent Java source for the Clojure code is to AOT-compile namespaces and then decompile the bytecodes into equivalent Java sources, using a Java bytecode decompiler.

There are several commercial and open source Java bytecode decompilers available. One of the open source decompilers we will discuss here is **JD-GUI**, which you can download from its website (http://jd.benow.ca/#jd-gui). Use a version suitable for your operating system.

Creating a new project

Let's see how exactly to arrive at the equivalent Java source code from Clojure. Create a new project using Leiningen: `lein new foo`. Then edit the `src/foo/core.clj` file with a `mul` function to find out the product of two numbers:

```
(ns foo.core)

(defn mul [x y]
  (* x y))
```

Compiling the Clojure sources into Java bytecode

Now, to compile Clojure sources into bytecodes and output them as `.class` files, run the `lein compile :all` command. It creates the `.class` files in the `target/classes` directory of the project as follows:

```
target/classes/
`-- foo
    |-- core$fn__18.class
    |-- core__init.class
    |-- core$loading__4910__auto__.class
    `-- core$mul.class
```

You can see that the `foo.core` namespace has been compiled into four `.class` files.

Decompiling the .class files into Java source

Assuming that you have already installed JD-GUI, decompiling the `.class` files is as simple as opening them using the JD-GUI application.

On inspection, the code for the `foo.core/mul` function looks as follows:

```
package foo;

import clojure.lang.AFunction;
import clojure.lang.Numbers;
import clojure.lang.RT;
import clojure.lang.Var;

public final class core$mul extends AFunction
{
   public static final Var const__0 = (Var)RT.var("clojure.core", "*");

   public Object invoke(Object x, Object y) { x = null; y = null;
return Numbers.multiply(x, y);
   }
}
```

It is easy to understand from the decompiled Java source that the foo.core/mul function is an instance of the core$mul class in the foo package extending the clojure. lang.AFunction class. We can also see that the argument types are of the Object type in method invoke(Object, Object), which implies the numbers will be boxed. In a similar fashion, you can decompile class files of any Clojure code to inspect the equivalent Java code. If you can combine this with knowledge about Java types and potential reflection and boxing, you can find the suboptimal spots in code and focus on what to improve upon.

Compiling the Clojure source without locals clearing

Note the Java code in the method invoke where it says x = null; y = null; — how is it possible that the code throws away the arguments, sets them to null, and effectively multiplies two null objects? This misleading decompilation happens due to locals clearing, a feature of the JVM bytecode implementation of Clojure, which has no equivalent in the Java language.

Starting with Clojure 1.4, the compiler supports the :disable-locals-clearing key in the dynamic clojure.core/*compiler-options* var that we cannot configure in the project.clj file. So, we cannot use the lein compile command, but we can start a **REPL** with the lein repl command to compile the classes:

```
user=> (binding [*compiler-options* {:disable-locals-clearing true}]
(compile 'foo.core))
foo.core
```

This generates the class files in the same location as we saw earlier in this section, but without x = null; y = null; because locals clearing is omitted.

Numerics, boxing, and primitives

Numerics are scalars. The discussion on numerics was deferred till this chapter for the sole reason that the numerics implementation in Clojure has strong Java underpinnings. Since version 1.3, Clojure has settled with 64-bit numerics as the default. Now, long and double are idiomatic and the default numeric types. Note that these are primitive Java types, not objects. Primitives in Java lead to high performance and have several optimizations associated with them at compiler and runtime levels. A local primitive is created on the stack (hence does not contribute to heap allocation and GC) and can be accessed directly without any kind of dereferencing. In Java, there also exist object equivalents of the numeric primitives, known as **boxed numerics** — these are regular objects that are allocated on the heap. The boxed numerics are also immutable objects, which mean not only does the JVM need to dereference the stored value when reading it, but also needs to create a new boxed object when a new value needs to be created.

It should be obvious that boxed numerics are slower than their primitive equivalents. The Oracle HotSpot JVM, when started with the `-server` option, aggressively inlines those functions (on frequent invocation) that contain a call to primitive operations. Clojure automatically uses **primitive numerics** at several levels. In the `let` blocks, `loop` blocks, arrays, and arithmetic operations (`+`, `-`, `*`, `/`, `inc`, `dec`, `<`, `<=`, `>`, `>=`), primitive numerics are detected and retained. The following table describes the primitive numerics with their boxed equivalents:

Primitive numeric type	Boxed equivalent
byte (1 byte)	`java.lang.Byte`
short (2 bytes)	`java.lang.Short`
int (4 bytes)	`java.lang.Integer`
float (4 bytes)	`java.lang.Float`
long (8 bytes)	`java.lang.Long`
double (8 bytes)	`java.lang.Double`

In Clojure, sometimes you may find the numerics are passed or returned as boxed objects to or from functions due to the lack of type information at runtime. Even if you have no control over such functions, you can coerce the values to be treated as primitives. The `byte`, `short`, `int`, `float`, `long`, and `double` functions create primitive equivalents from given boxed numeric values.

One of the Lisp traditions is to provide correct (http://en.wikipedia.org/wiki/Numerical_tower) arithmetic implementation. A lower type should not truncate values when overflow or underflow happens, but rather should be promoted to construct a higher type to maintain correctness. Clojure follows this constraint and provides **autopromotion** via prime (http://en.wikipedia.org/wiki/Prime_(symbol)) functions: `+'`, `-'`, `*'`, `inc'`, and `dec'`. Autopromotion provides correctness at the cost of some performance.

There are also arbitrary length or precision numeric types in Clojure that let us store unbounded numbers but have poorer performance compared to primitives. The `bigint` and `bigdec` functions let us create numbers of arbitrary length and precision.

If we try to carry out any operations with primitive numerics that may result in a number beyond its maximum capacity, the operation maintains correctness by throwing an exception. On the other hand, when we use the prime functions, they autopromote to provide correctness. There is another set of operations called unchecked operations, which do not check for overflow or underflow and can potentially return incorrect results.

In some cases, they may be faster than regular and prime functions. Such functions are unchecked-add, unchecked-subtract, unchecked-multiply, unchecked-divide, unchecked-inc, and unchecked-dec. We can also enable unchecked math behavior for regular arithmetic functions using the *unchecked-math* var; simply include the following in your source code file:

```
(set! *unchecked-math* true)
```

One of the common needs in the arithmetic is the division used to find out the quotient and remainder after a natural number division. Clojure's / function provides a rational number division yielding a ratio, and the mod function provides a true modular arithmetic division. These functions are slower than the quot and rem functions that compute the division quotient and the remainder, respectively.

Arrays

Besides objects and primitives, Java has a special type of collection storage structure called **arrays**. Once created, arrays cannot be grown or shrunk without copying data and creating another array to hold the result. Array elements are always homogeneous in type. The array elements are similar to places where you can mutate them to hold new values. Unlike collections such as list and vector, arrays can contain primitive elements, which make them a very fast storage mechanism without GC overhead.

Arrays often form a basis for mutable data structures. For example, Java's java.lang.ArrayList implementation uses arrays internally. In Clojure, arrays can be used for fast numeric storage and processing, efficient algorithms, and so on. Unlike collections, arrays can have one or more dimensions. So you could layout data in an array such as a matrix or cube. Let's see Clojure's support for arrays:

Description	Example	Notes
Create array	(make-array Integer 20)	Array of type (boxed) integer
	(make-array Integer/ TYPE 20)	Array of primitive type integer
	(make-array Long/TYPE 20 10)	Two-dimensional array of primitive long
Create array of primitives	(int-array 20)	Array of primitive integer of size 20
	(int-array [10 20 30 40])	Array of primitive integer created from a vector
Create array from coll	(to-array [10 20 30 40])	Array from sequable

Description	Example	Notes
	`(to-array-2d [[10 20 30][40 50 60]])`	Two-dimensional array from collection
Clone an array	`(aclone (to-array [:a :b :c]))`	
Get array element	`(aget array-object 0 3)`	Get element at index [0][3] in a 2-D array
Mutate array element	`(aset array-object 0 3 :foo)`	Set obj :foo at index [0][3] in a 2-D array
Mutate primitive array element	`(aset-int int-array-object 2 6 89)`	Set value 89 at index [2][6] in 2-D array
Find length of array	`(alength array-object)`	`alength` is significantly faster than count

Map over an array	`(def a (int-array [10 20 30 40 50 60]))`
	`(seq`
	`    (amap a idx ret`
	`        (do (println idx (seq ret))`
	`            (inc (aget a idx)))))`
		Unlike map, `amap` returns a non-lazy array, which is significantly faster over array elements. Note that `amap` is faster only when properly type hinted. See next section for type hinting.

Reduce over an array	`(def a (int-array [10 20 30 40 50 60]))`
	`(areduce a idx ret 0`
	`    (do (println idx ret)`
	`        (+ ret idx)))`
		Unlike reduce, `areduce` is significantly faster over array elements. Note that reduce is faster only when properly type hinted. See next section for type hinting.

Cast to primitive arrays	`(ints int-array-object)`	Used with type hinting (see next section)

Like `int-array` and `ints`, there are functions for other types as well:

Array construction function	Primitive-array casting function	Type hinting (does not work for vars)	Generic array type hinting
boolean-array	booleans	`^booleans`	`^"[Z"`
byte-array	bytes	`^bytes`	`^"[B"`
short-array	shorts	`^shorts`	`^"[S"`
char-array	chars	`^chars`	`^"[C"`

Array construction function	Primitive-array casting function	Type hinting (does not work for vars)	Generic array type hinting
int-array	ints	^ints	^"[I"
long-array	longs	^longs	^"[J"
float-array	floats	^floats	^"[F"
double-array	doubles	^doubles	^"[D"
object-array	--	^objects	^"[Ljava.lang.Object"

Arrays are favored over other data structures mainly due to performance, and sometimes due to interop. Extreme care should be taken to type hint the arrays and use the appropriate functions to work with them.

Reflection and type hints

Sometimes, as Clojure is dynamically typed, the Clojure compiler is unable to figure out the type of object to invoke a certain method. In such cases, Clojure uses **reflection**, which is considerably slower than the direct method dispatch. Clojure's solution to this is something called **type hints**. Type hints are a way to annotate arguments and objects with static types, so that the Clojure compiler can emit bytecodes for efficient dispatch.

The easiest way to know where to put type hints is to turn on reflection warning in the code. Consider this code that determines the length of a string:

```
user=> (set! *warn-on-reflection* true)
true
user=> (def s "Hello, there")
#'user/s
user=> (.length s)
Reflection warning, NO_SOURCE_PATH:1 - reference to field length can't
be resolved.
12
user=> (defn str-len [^String s] (.length s))
#'user/str-len
user=> (str-len s)
12
user=> (.length ^String s)  ; type hint when passing argument
12
```

```
user=> (def ^String t "Hello, there")   ; type hint at var level
#'user/t
user=> (.length t)   ; no more reflection warning
12
user=> (time (dotimes [_ 1000000] (.length s)))
Reflection warning, /private/var/folders/cv/myzdv_
vd675g4l7y92jx9bm5lflvxq/T/form-init6904047906685577265.clj:1:28 -
reference to field length can't be resolved.
"Elapsed time: 2409.155848 msecs"
nil
user=> (time (dotimes [_ 1000000] (.length t)))
"Elapsed time: 12.991328 msecs"
nil
```

In the previous snippet, we can clearly see there is a very big difference in performance in the code that uses reflection versus the code that does not. When working on a project, you may want reflection warning to be turned on for all files. You can do it easily in Leiningen. Just put the following entry in your `project.clj` file:

```
:profiles {:dev {:global-vars {*warn-on-reflection* true}}}
```

This will automatically turn on warning reflection every time you begin any kind of invocation via Leiningen in the dev workflow such as REPL and test.

An array of primitives

Recall the examples on `amap` and `areduce` from the previous section. If we run them with reflection warning on, we'd be warned that it uses reflection. Let's type hint them:

```
(def a (int-array [10 20 30 40 50 60]))
;; amap example
(seq
  (amap ^ints a idx ret
    (do (println idx (seq ret))
      (inc (aget ^ints a idx)))))
;; areduce example
(areduce ^ints a idx ret 0
  (do (println idx ret)
    (+ ret idx)))
```

Note that the primitive array hint `^ints` does not work at the var level. So, it would not work if you defined the var `a`, as in the following:

```
(def ^ints a (int-array [10 20 30 40 50 60]))  ; wrong, will complain
later
(def ^"[I" a (int-array [10 20 30 40 50 60]))  ; correct
(def ^{:tag 'ints} a (int-array [10 20 30 40 50 60])) ; correct
```

This notation is for an array of integers. Other primitive array types have similar type hints. Refer to the previous section for type hinting for various primitive array types.

Primitives

The type hinting of primitive locals is neither required nor allowed. However, you can type hint function arguments as primitives. Clojure allows up to four arguments in functions to be type hinted:

```
(defn do-something
  [^long a ^long b ^long c ^long d]
  ..)
```

 Boxing may result in something not always being a primitive. In those cases, you can coerce those using respective primitive types.

Macros and metadata

In macros, type hinting does not work the way it does in the other parts of the code. Since macros are about transforming the **Abstract Syntax Tree (AST)**, we need to have a mental map of the transformation and we should add type hints as metadata in the code. For example, if `str-len` is a macro to find the length of a string, we make use of the following code:

```
(defmacro str-len
  [s]
  `(.length ~(with-meta s {:tag String})))
;; below is another way to write the same macro
(defmacro str-len
  [s]
  `(.length ~(vary-meta s assoc :tag `String)))
```

In the preceding code, we alter the metadata of the symbol s by tagging it with the type `String`, which happens to be the `java.lang.String` class in this case. For array types, we can use `[Ljava.lang.String` for an array of string objects and similarly for others. If you try to use `str-len` listed previously, you may notice this works only when we pass the string bound to a local or a var, not as a string literal. To mitigate this, we can write the macro as follows:

```
(defmacro str-len
  [s]
  `(let [^String s# ~s] (.length s#)))
```

Here we bind the argument to a type-hinted gensym local, hence calling `.length` on it does not use reflection and there is no reflection warning emitted as such.

Type hinting via metadata also works with functions, albeit in a different notation:

```
(defn foo [] "Hello")
(defn foo ^String [] "Hello")
(defn foo
  (^String [] "Hello")
  (^String [x] (str "Hello, " x)))
```

Except for the first example in the preceding snippet, they are type hinted to return the `java.lang.String` type.

String concatenation

The `str` function in Clojure is used to concatenate and convert to string tokens. In Java, when we write `"hello" + e`, the Java compiler translates this to an equivalent code that uses `StringBuilder` and is considerably faster than the `str` function in micro-benchmarks. To obtain close-to-Java performance, in Clojure we can use a similar mechanism with a macro directly using Java interop to avoid the indirection via the `str` function. The **Stringer** (`https://github.com/kumarshantanu/stringer`) library adopts the same technique to come up with fast string concatenation in Clojure:

```
(require '[stringer.core :as s])
user=> (time (dotimes [_ 10000000] (str "foo" :bar 707 nil 'baz)))
"Elapsed time: 2044.284333 msecs"
nil
user=> (time (dotimes [_ 10000000] (s/strcat "foo" :bar 707 nil
'baz)))
"Elapsed time: 555.843271 msecs"
nil
```

Here, Stringer also aggressively concatenates the literals during the compile phase.

Miscellaneous

In a type (as in `deftype`), the mutable instance variables can be optionally annotated as `^:volatile-mutable` or `^:unsynchronized-mutable`. For example:

```
(deftype Counter [^:volatile-mutable ^long now]
  ..)
```

Unlike `defprotocol`, the `definterface` macro lets us provide a return type hint for methods:

```
(definterface Foo
  (^long doSomething [^long a ^double b]))
```

The `proxy-super` macro (which is used inside the `proxy` macro) is a special case where you cannot directly apply a type hint. The reason being that it relies on the implicit this object that is automatically created by the `proxy` macro. In this case, you must explicitly bind this to a type:

```
(proxy [Object] []
  (equals [other]
    (let [^Object this this]
      (proxy-super equals other))))
```

Type hinting is quite important for performance in Clojure. Fortunately, we need to type hint only when required and it's easy to find out when. In many cases, a gain from type hinting overshadows the gains from code inlining.

Using array/numeric libraries for efficiency

You may have noticed in the previous sections, when working with numerics, performance depends a lot on whether the data is based on arrays and primitives. It may take a lot of meticulousness on the programmer's part to correctly coerce data into primitives and arrays at all stages of the computation in order to achieve optimum efficiency. Fortunately, the high-performance enthusiasts from the Clojure community realized this issue early on and created some dedicated open source libraries to mitigate the problem.

HipHip

HipHip is a Clojure library used to work with arrays of primitive types. It provides a safety net, that is, it strictly accepts only primitive array arguments to work with. As a result, passing silently boxed primitive arrays as arguments always results in an exception. HipHip macros and functions rarely need the programmer to type hint anything during the operations. It supports arrays of primitive types such as `int`, `long`, `float`, and `double`.

The HipHip project is available at `https://github.com/Prismatic/hiphip`.

As of writing, HipHip's most recent version is 0.2.0 that supports Clojure 1.5.x or above, and is tagged as an Alpha release. There is a standard set of operations provided by HipHip for arrays of all of the four primitive types: integer array operations are in the namespace `hiphip.int`; double precision array operations in `hiphip.double`; and so on. The operations are all type hinted for the respective types. All of the operations for `int`, `long`, `float`, and `double` in respective namespaces are essentially the same except for the array type:

Category	Function/macro	Description
Core functions	`aclone`	Like `clojure.core/aclone`, for primitives
	`alength`	Like `clojure.core/alength`, for primitives
	`aget`	Like `clojure.core/aget`, for primitives
	`aset`	Like `clojure.core/aset`, for primitives
	`ainc`	Increment array element by specified value
Equiv hiphip. array operations	`amake`	Make a new array and fill values computed by expression
	`areduce`	Like `clojure.core/areduce`, with HipHip array bindings
	`doarr`	Like `clojure.core/doseq`, with HipHip array bindings
	`amap`	Like `clojure.core/for`, creates new array
	`afill!`	Like preceding `amap`, but overwrites array argument
Mathy operations	`asum`	Compute sum of array elements using expression
	`aproduct`	Compute product of array elements using expression
	`amean`	Compute mean over array elements
	`dot-product`	Compute dot product of two arrays

Category	Function/macro	Description
Finding minimum/ maximum, Sorting	amax-index	Find maximum value in array and return the index
	amax	Find maximum value in array and return it
	amin-index	Find minimum value in array and return the index
	amin	Find minimum value in array and return it
	apartition!	Three-way partition of array: less, equal, greater than pivot
	aselect!	Gather smallest k elements at the beginning of array
	asort!	Sort array in-place using Java's built-in implementation
	asort-max!	Partial in-place sort gathering top k elements to the end
	asort-min!	Partial in-place sort gathering min k elements to the top
	apartition-indices!	Like apartition! but mutates index-array instead of values
	aselect-indices!	Like aselect! but mutates index-array instead of values
	asort-indices!	Like asort! but mutates index-array instead of values
	amax-indices	Get index-array; last k indices pointing to max k values
	amin-indices	Get index-array; first k indices pointing to min k values

To include HipHip as a dependency in your Leiningen project, specify it in project.clj:

```
:dependencies [;; other dependencies
               [prismatic/hiphip "0.2.0"]]
```

As an example of how to use HipHip, let's see how to compute the normalized values of an array:

```
(require '[hiphip.double :as hd])

(def xs (double-array [12.3 23.4 34.5 45.6 56.7 67.8]))

(let [s (hd/asum xs)] (hd/amap [x xs] (/ x s)))
```

Unless we make sure that xs is an array of primitive doubles, HipHip will throw ClassCastException when the type is incorrect, and IllegalArgumentException in other cases. I recommend exploring the HipHip project to gain more insight into using it effectively.

primitive-math

We can set *warn-on-reflection* to true to let Clojure warn us when the reflection is used at invocation boundaries. However, when Clojure has to implicitly use reflection to perform math, the only resort is to either use a profiler or compile the Clojure source down to bytecode, and analyze boxing and reflection with a decompiler. This is where the primitive-math library helps, by producing extra warnings and throwing exceptions.

The primitive-math library is available at https://github.com/ztellman/primitive-math.

As of writing, primitive-math is at version 0.1.4; you can include it as a dependency in your Leiningen project by editing project.clj as follows:

```
:dependencies [;; other dependencies
               [primitive-math "0.1.4"]]
```

The following code is how it can be used (recall the example from the *Decompiling the .class files into Java source* section):

```
;; must enable reflection warnings for extra warnings from primitive-
math
(set! *warn-on-reflection* true)
(require '[primitive-math :as pm])
(defn mul [x y] (pm/* x y))   ; primitive-math produces reflection
warning
(mul 10.3 2)                           ; throws exception
(defn mul [^long x ^long y] (pm/* x y))  ; no warning after type
hinting
(mul 10.3 2)   ; returns 20
```

While primitive-math is a useful library, the problem it solves is mostly taken care of by the boxing detection feature in Clojure 1.7 (see next section *Detecting boxed math*). However, this library is still useful if you are unable to use Clojure 1.7 or higher.

Detecting boxed math

Boxed math is hard to detect and is a source of performance issues. Clojure 1.7 introduces a way to warn the user when boxed math happens. This can be configured in the following way:

```
(set! *unchecked-math* :warn-on-boxed)

(defn sum-till [n] (/ (* n (inc n)) 2))   ; causes warning
Boxed math warning, /private/var/folders/cv/myzdv_
vd675g4l7y92jx9bm5lflvxq/T/form-init3701519533014890866.clj:1:28 -
call: public static java.lang.Number clojure.lang.Numbers.unchecked_
inc(java.lang.Object).
Boxed math warning, /private/var/folders/cv/myzdv_
vd675g4l7y92jx9bm5lflvxq/T/form-init3701519533014890866.clj:1:23 -
call: public static java.lang.Number clojure.lang.Numbers.unchecked_
multiply(java.lang.Object,java.lang.Object).
Boxed math warning, /private/var/folders/cv/myzdv_
vd675g4l7y92jx9bm5lflvxq/T/form-init3701519533014890866.clj:1:20 -
call: public static java.lang.Number clojure.lang.Numbers.divide(java.
lang.Object,long).

;; now we define again with type hint
(defn sum-till [^long n] (/ (* n (inc n)) 2))
```

When working with Leiningen, you can enable boxed math warnings by putting the following entry in the `project.clj` file:

```
:global-vars {*unchecked-math* :warn-on-boxed}
```

The math operations in `primitive-math` (like HipHip) are implemented via macros. Therefore, they cannot be used as higher order functions and, as a consequence, may not compose well with other code. I recommend exploring the project to see what suits your program use case. Adopting Clojure 1.7 obviates the boxing discovery issues by means of a boxed-warning feature.

Resorting to Java and native code

In a handful of cases, where the lack of imperative, stack-based, mutable variables in Clojure may make the code not perform as well as Java, we may need to evaluate alternatives to make it faster. I would advise you to consider writing such code directly in Java for better performance.

Another consideration is to use native OS capabilities, such as memory-mapped buffers (`http://docs.oracle.com/javase/7/docs/api/java/nio/MappedByteBuffer.html`) or files and unsafe operations (`http://highlyscalable.wordpress.com/2012/02/02/direct-memory-access-in-java/`). Note that unsafe operations are potentially hazardous and not recommended in general. Such times are also an opportunity to consider writing performance-critical pieces of code in C or C++ and then access them via the **Java Native Interface (JNI)**.

Proteus – mutable locals in Clojure

Proteus is an open source Clojure library that lets you treat a local as a local variable, thereby allowing its unsynchronized mutation within the local scope only. Note that this library depends on the internal implementation structure of Clojure as of Clojure 1.5.1. The **Proteus** project is available at `https://github.com/ztellman/proteus`.

You can include Proteus as a dependency in the Leiningen project by editing `project.clj`:

```
:dependencies [;;other dependencies
               [proteus "0.1.4"]]
```

Using Proteus in code is straightforward, as shown in the following code snippet:

```
(require '[proteus :as p])
(p/let-mutable [a 10]
  (println a)
  (set! a 20)
  (println a))
;; Output below:
;; 10
;; 20
```

Since Proteus allows mutation only in the local scope, the following throws an exception:

```
(p/let-mutable [a 10 add2! (fn [x] (set! x (+ 2 x)))]
  (add2! a)
  (println a))
```

The mutable locals are very fast and may be quite useful in tight loops. Proteus is unconventional by Clojure idioms, but it may give the required performance boost without having to write Java code.

Summary

Clojure has strong Java interoperability and underpinning, due to which programmers can leverage the performance benefits nearing those of Java. For performance-critical code, it is sometimes necessary to understand how Clojure interacts with Java and how to turn the right knobs. Numerics is a key area where Java interoperability is required to get optimum performance. Type hints are another important performance trick that is frequently useful. There are several open source Clojure libraries that make such activities easier for the programmer.

In the next chapter, we will dig deeper below Java and see how the hardware and the JVM stack play a key role in offering the performance we get, what their constraints are, and how to use their understanding to get better performance.

4
Host Performance

In the previous chapters, we noted how Clojure interoperates with Java. In this chapter we will go a bit deeper to understand the internals better. We will touch upon several layers of the entire stack, but our major focus will be the JVM, in particular the Oracle HotSpot JVM, though there are several JVM vendors to choose from (http://en.wikipedia.org/wiki/List_of_Java_virtual_machines). At the time of writing this, Oracle JDK 1.8 is the latest stable release and early OpenJDK 1.9 builds are available. In this chapter we will discuss:

- How the hardware subsystems function from the performance viewpoint
- Organization of the JVM internals and how that is related to performance
- How to measure the amount of space occupied by various objects in the heap
- Profile Clojure code for latency using Criterium

The hardware

There are various hardware components that may impact the performance of software in different ways. The processors, caches, memory subsystem, I/O subsystems, and so on, all have varying degrees of performance impact depending upon the use cases. In the following sections we look into each of those aspects.

Processors

Since about the late 1980s, microprocessors have been employing pipelining and instruction-level parallelism to speed up their performance. Processing an instruction at the CPU level consists of typically four cycles: **fetch**, **decode**, **execute**, and **writeback**. Modern processors optimize the cycles by running them in parallel— while one instruction is executed, the next instruction is being decoded, and the one after that is being fetched, and so on. This style is called **instruction pipelining**.

In practice, in order to speed up execution even further, the stages are subdivided into many shorter stages, thus leading to deeper super-pipeline architecture. The length of the longest stage in the pipeline limits the clock speed of the CPU. By splitting stages into substages, the processor can be run at a higher clock speed, where more cycles are required for each instruction, but the processor still completes one instruction per cycle. Since there are more cycles per second now, we get better performance in terms of throughput per second even though the latency of each instruction is now higher.

Branch prediction

The processor must fetch and decode instructions in advance even when it encounters instructions of the conditional if-then form. Consider an equivalent of the (if (test a) (foo a) (bar a)) Clojure expression. The processor must choose a branch to fetch and decode, the question is should it fetch the if branch or the else branch? Here, the processor makes a guess as to which instruction to fetch/decode. If the guess turns out to be correct, it is a performance gain as usual; otherwise, the processor has to throw away the result of the fetch/decode process and start on the other branch afresh.

Processors deal with branch prediction using an on-chip branch prediction table. It contains recent code branches and two bits per branch, indicating whether or not the branch was taken, while also accommodating one-off, not-taken occurrences.

Today, branch prediction is extremely important in processors for performance, so modern processors dedicate hardware resources and special predication instructions to improve the prediction accuracy and lower the cost of a mispredict penalty.

Instruction scheduling

High-latency instructions and branching usually lead to empty cycles in the instruction pipeline known as **stalls** or **bubbles**. These cycles are often used to do other work by the means of instruction reordering. Instruction reordering is implemented at the hardware level via out of order execution and at the compiler level via compile time instruction scheduling (also called **static instruction scheduling**).

The processor needs to remember the dependencies between instructions when carrying out the out-of-order execution. This cost is somewhat mitigated by using renamed registers, wherein register values are stored into / loaded from memory locations, potentially on different physical registers, so that they can be executed in parallel. This necessitates that out-of-order processors always maintain a mapping of instructions and corresponding registers they use, which makes their design complex and power hungry. With a few exceptions, almost all high-performance CPUs today have out-of-order designs.

Good compilers are usually extremely aware of processors, and are capable of optimizing the code by rearranging processor instructions in a way that there are fewer bubbles in the processor instruction pipeline. A few high-performance CPUs still rely on only static instruction reordering instead of out-of-order instruction reordering and, in turn, save chip area due to simpler design—the saved area is used to accommodate extra cache or CPU cores. Low-power processors, such as those from the ARM and Atom family, use in-order design. Unlike most CPUs, the modern GPUs use in-order design with deep pipelines, which is compensated by very fast context switching. This leads to high latency and high throughput on GPUs.

Threads and cores

Concurrency and parallelism via context switches, hardware threads, and cores are very common today and we have accepted them as a norm to implement in our programs. However, we should understand why we needed such a design in the first place. Most of the real-world code we write today does not have more than a modest scope for instruction-level parallelism. Even with hardware-based, out-of-order execution and static instruction reordering, no more than two instructions per cycle are truly parallel. Hence, another potential source of instructions that can be pipelined and executed in parallel are the programs other than the currently running one.

The empty cycles in a pipeline can be dedicated to other running programs, which assume that there are other currently running programs that need the processor's attention. **Simultaneous multithreading (SMT)** is a hardware design that enables such kinds of parallelism. Intel implements SMT named as **HyperThreading** in some of its processors. While SMT presents a single physical processor as two or more logical processors, a true multiprocessor system executes one thread per processor, thus achieving simultaneous execution. A multicore processor includes two or more processors per chip, but has the properties of a multiprocessor system.

In general, multicore processors significantly outperform SMT processors. Performance on SMT processors can vary by the use case. It peaks in those cases where code is highly variable or threads do not compete for the same hardware resources, and dips when the threads are cache-bound on the same processor. What is also important is that some programs are simply not inherently parallel. In such cases it may be hard to make them go faster without the explicit use of threads in the program.

Memory systems

It is important to understand the memory performance characteristics to know the likely impact on the programs we write. Data-intensive programs that are also inherently parallel, such as audio/video processing and scientific computation, are largely limited by memory bandwidth, not by the processor. Adding processors would not make them faster unless the memory bandwidth is also increased. Consider another class of programs, such as 3D graphics rendering or database systems that are limited mainly by memory latency but not the memory bandwidth. SMT can be highly suitable for such programs, where threads do not compete for the same hardware resources.

Memory access roughly constitutes a quarter of all instructions executed by a processor. A code block typically begins with memory-load instructions and the remainder portion depends on the loaded data. This stalls the instructions and prevents large-scale, instruction-level parallelism. As if that was not bad enough, even superscalar processors (which can issue more than one instruction per clock cycle) can issue, at most, two memory instructions per cycle. Building fast memory systems is limited by natural factors such as the speed of light. It impacts the signal round trip to the RAM. This is a natural hard limit and any optimization can only work around it.

Data transfer between the processor and motherboard chipset is one of the factors that induce memory latency. This is countered using a **faster front-side bus (FSB)**. Nowadays, most modern processors fix this problem by integrating the memory controller directly at the chip level. The significant difference between the processor versus memory latencies is known as the **memory wall**. This has plateaued in recent times due to processor clock speeds hitting power and heat limits, but notwithstanding this, memory latency continues to be a significant problem.

Unlike CPUs, GPUs typically realize a sustained high-memory bandwidth. Due to latency hiding, they utilize the bandwidth even during a high number-crunching workload.

Cache

To overcome the memory latency, modern processors employ a special type of very fast memory placed onto the processor chip or close to the chip. The purpose of the cache is to store the most recently used data from the memory. Caches are of different levels: **L1** cache is located on the processor chip; **L2** cache is bigger and located farther away from the processor compared to L1. There is often an **L3** cache, which is even bigger and located farther from the processor than L2. In Intel's Haswell processor, the L1 cache is generally 64 kilobytes (32 KB instruction plus 32 KB data) in size, L2 is 256 KB per core, and L3 is 8 MB.

While memory latency is very bad, fortunately caches seem to work very well. The L1 cache is much faster than accessing the main memory. The reported cache hit rates in real-world programs is 90 percent, which makes a strong case for caches. A cache works like a dictionary of memory addresses to a block of data values. Since the value is a block of memory, the caching of adjacent memory locations has mostly no additional overhead. Note that L2 is slower and bigger than L1, and L3 is slower and bigger than L2. On Intel Sandybridge processors, register lookup is instantaneous; L1 cache lookup takes three clock cycles, L2 takes nine, L3 takes 21, and main memory access takes 150 to 400 clock cycles.

Interconnect

A processor communicates with the memory and other processors via interconnect that are generally of two types of architecture: **Symmetric multiprocessing (SMP)** and **Non-uniform memory access (NUMA)**. In SMP, a bus interconnects processors and memory with the help of bus controllers. The bus acts as a broadcast device for the end points. The bus often becomes a bottleneck with a large number of processors and memory banks. SMP systems are cheaper to build and harder to scale to a large number of cores compared to NUMA. In a NUMA system, collections of processors and memory are connected point to point to other such groups of processors and memory. Every such group is called a node. Local memory of a node is accessible by other nodes and vice versa. Intel's **HyperTransport** and **QuickPath** interconnect technologies support NUMA.

Storage and networking

Storage and networking are the most commonly used hardware components besides the processor, cache, and memory. Many of the real-world applications are more often I/O bound than execution-bound. Such I/O technologies are continuously advancing and there is a wide variety of components available in the market. The consideration of such devices should be based on the exact performance and reliability characteristics for the use case. Another important criterion is to know how well they are supported by the target operating system drivers. Current day storage technologies mostly build upon hard disks and solid state drives. The applicability of network devices and protocols vary widely as per the business use case. A detailed discussion of I/O hardware is beyond the scope of this book.

The Java Virtual Machine

The Java Virtual Machine is a bytecode-oriented, garbage-collected virtual machine that specifies its own instruction set. The instructions have equivalent bytecodes that are interpreted and compiled to the underlying OS and hardware by the **Java Runtime Environment** (**JRE**). Objects are referred to using symbolic references. The data types in the JVM are fully standardized as a single spec across all JVM implementations on all platforms and architectures. The JVM also follows the network byte order, which means communication between Java programs on different architectures can happen using the big-endian byte order. **Jvmtop** (`https://code.google.com/p/jvmtop/`) is a handy JVM monitoring tool similar to the top command in Unix-like systems.

The just-in-time compiler

The **just-in-time** (**JIT**) compiler is part of the JVM. When the JVM starts up, the JIT compiler knows hardly anything about the running code so it simply interprets the JVM bytecodes. As the program keeps running, the JIT compiler starts profiling the code by collecting statistics and analyzing the call and bytecode patterns. When a method call count exceeds a certain threshold, the JIT compiler applies a number of optimizations to the code. Most common optimizations are inlining and native code generating. The final and static methods and classes are great candidates for inlining. JIT compilation does not come without a cost; it occupies memory to store the profiled code and sometimes it has to revert the wrong speculative optimization. However, JIT compilation is almost always amortized over a long duration of code execution. In rare cases, turning off JIT compilation may be useful if either the code is too large or there are no hotspots in the code due to infrequent execution.

A JRE has typically two kinds of JIT compilers: client and server. Which JIT compiler is used by default depends on the type of hardware and platform. The client JIT compiler is meant for client programs such as command-line and desktop applications. We can start the JRE with the `-server` option to invoke the server JIT compiler, which is really meant for long-running programs on a server. The threshold for JIT compilation is higher in the server than the client. The difference in the two kinds of JIT compilers is that the client targets upfront, visible lower latency, and the server is assumed to be running on a high-resource hardware and tries to optimize for throughput.

The JIT compiler in the Oracle HotSpot JVM observes the code execution to determine the most frequently invoked methods, which are hotspots. Such hotspots are usually just a fraction of the entire code that can be cheap to focus on and optimize. The **HotSpot JIT** compiler is lazy and adaptive. It is lazy because it compiles only those methods to native code that have crossed a certain threshold, and not all the code that it encounters. Compiling to native code is a time-consuming process and compiling all code would be wasteful. It is adaptive to gradually increasing the aggressiveness of its compilation on frequently called code, which implies that the code is not optimized only once but many times over as the code gets executed repeatedly. After a method call crosses the first JIT compiler threshold, it is optimized and the counter is reset to zero. At the same time, the optimization count for the code is set to one. When the call exceeds the threshold yet again, the counter is reset to zero and the optimization count is incremented; and this time a more aggressive optimization is applied. This cycle continues until the code cannot be optimized anymore.

The HotSpot JIT compiler does a whole bunch of optimizations. Some of the most prominent ones are as follows:

- **Inlining**: Inlining of methods—very small methods, the static and final methods, methods in final classes, and small methods involving only primitive numerics are prime candidates for inlining.

- **Lock elimination**: Locking is a performance overhead. Fortunately, if the lock object monitor is not reachable from other threads, the lock is eliminated.

- **Virtual call elimination**: Often, there is only one implementation for an interface in a program. The JIT compiler eliminates the virtual call and replaces that with a direct method call on the class implementation object.

- **Non-volatile memory write elimination**: The non-volatile data members and references in an object are not guaranteed to be visible by the threads other than the current thread. This criterion is utilized not to update such references in memory and rather use hardware registers or the stack via native code.

- **Native code generation**: The JIT compiler generates native code for frequently invoked methods together with the arguments. The generated native code is stored in the code cache.

- **Control flow and local optimizations**: The JIT compiler frequently reorders and splits the code for better performance. It also analyzes the branching of control and optimizes code based on that.

There should rarely be any reason to disable JIT compilation, but it can be done by passing the `-Djava.compiler=NONE` parameter when starting the JRE. The default compile threshold can be changed by passing `-XX:CompileThreshold=9800` to the JRE executable where `9800` is the example threshold. The `XX:+PrintCompilation` and `-XX:-CITime` options make the JIT compiler print the JIT statistics and time spent on JIT.

Memory organization

The memory used by the JVM is divided into several segments. JVM, being a stack-based execution model, one of the memory segments is the stack area. Every thread is given a stack where the stack frames are stored in **Last-in-First-out (LIFO)** order. The stack includes a **program counter (PC)** that points to the instruction in the JVM memory currently being executed. When a method is called, a new stack frame is created containing the local variable array and the operand stack. Contrary to conventional stacks, the operand stack holds instructions to load local variable / field values and computation results — a mechanism that is also used to prepare method parameters before a call and to store the return value. The stack frame itself may be allocated on the heap. The easiest way to inspect the order of stack frames in the current thread is to execute the following code:

```
(require 'clojure.repl)
(clojure.repl/pst (Throwable.))
```

When a thread requires more stack space than what the JVM can provide, `StackOverflowError` is thrown.

The heap is the main memory area where the object and array allocations are done. It is shared across all JVM threads. The heap may be of a fixed size or expanding, depending on the arguments passed to the JRE on startup. Trying to allocate more heap space than what the JVM can make room for results in `OutOfMemoryError` to be thrown. The allocations in the heap are subject to garbage collection. When an object is no more reachable via any reference, it is garbage collected, with the notable exception of weak, soft, and phantom references. Objects pointed to by non-strong references take longer to GC.

The method area is logically a part of the heap memory and contains per-class structures such as the field and method information, runtime constant pool, code for method, and constructor bodies. It is shared across all JVM threads. In the Oracle HotSpot JVM (up to Version 7), the method area is found in a memory area called the **permanent generation**. In HotSpot Java 8, the permanent generation is replaced by a native memory area called **Metaspace**.

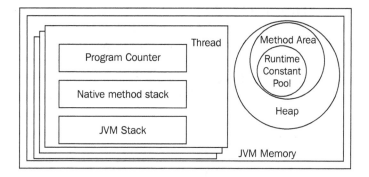

The JVM contains the native code and the Java bytecode to be provided to the Java API implementation and the JVM implementation. The native code call stack is maintained separately for each thread stack. The JVM stack contains the Java method calls. Please note that the JVM spec for Java SE 7 and 8 does not imply a native method stack, but for Java SE 5 and 6, it does.

HotSpot heap and garbage collection

The Oracle HotSpot JVM uses a generational heap. The three main generations are **Young**, **Tenured** (old), and **Perm** (permanent) (up to HotSpot JDK 1.7 only). As objects survive garbage collection, they move from **Eden** to **Survivor** and from **Survivor** to **Tenured** spaces. The new instances are allocated in the **Eden** segment, which is a very cheap operation (as cheap as a pointer bump, and faster than a C `malloc` call), if it already has sufficient free space. When the Eden area does not have enough free space, a minor GC is triggered. This copies the live objects from **Eden** into the **Survivor** space. In the same operation, live objects are checked in **Survivor-1** and copied over to **Survivor-2**, thus keeping the live objects only in **Survivor-2**. This scheme keeps **Eden** and **Survivor-1** empty and unfragmented to make new allocations, and is known as **copy collection**.

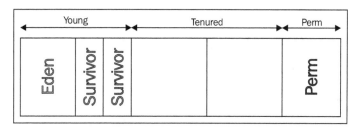

After a certain survival threshold in the young generation, the objects are moved to the tenured/old generation. If it is not possible to do a minor GC, a major GC is attempted. The major GC does not use copying, but rather relies on mark-and-sweep algorithms. We can use throughput collectors (**Serial**, **Parallel**, and **ParallelOld**) or low-pause collectors (**Concurrent** and **G1**) for the old generation. The following table shows a non-exhaustive list of options to be used for each collector type:

Collector name	JVM flag
Serial	-XX:+UseSerialGC
Parallel	-XX:+UseParallelGC
Parallel Compacting	-XX:+UseParallelOldGC
Concurrent	-XX:+UseConcMarkSweepGC
	-XX:+UseParNewGC
	-XX:+CMSParallelRemarkEnabled
G1	-XX:+UseG1GC

The previously mentioned flags can be used to start the Java runtime. For example, in the following command, we start the server JVM with a 4 GB heap using Parallel compacting GC:

```
java \
  -server \
  -Xms4096m -Xmx4096m \
  -XX:+UseParallelOldGC XX:ParallelGCThreads=4 \
  -jar application-standalone.jar
```

Sometimes, due to running full GC multiple times, the tenured space may have become so fragmented that it may not be feasible to move objects from Survivor to Tenured spaces. In those cases, a full GC with compaction is triggered. During this period, the application may appear unresponsive due to the full GC in action.

Measuring memory (heap/stack) usage

One of the prime reasons for a performance hit in the JVM is garbage collection. It certainly helps to know how heap memory is used by the objects we create and how to reduce the impact on GC by means of a lower footprint. Let's inspect how the representation of an object may lead to heap space.

Every (uncompressed) object or array reference on a 64-bit JVM is 16 bytes long. On a 32-bit JVM, every reference is 8 bytes long. As the 64-bit architecture is becoming more commonplace now, the 64-bit JVM is more likely to be used on servers. Fortunately, for a heap size of up to 32 GB, the JVM (Java 7) can use compressed pointers (default behavior) that are only 4 bytes in size. Java 8 VMs can address up to 64 GB heap size via compressed pointers as seen in the following table:

	Uncompressed	Compressed	32-bit
Reference (pointer)	8	4	4
Object header	16	12	8
Array header	24	16	12
Superclass padding	8	4	4

This table illustrates pointer sizes in different modes (reproduced with permission from Attila Szegedi: `http://www.slideshare.net/aszegedi/everything-i-ever-learned-about-jvm-performance-tuning-twitter/20`).

We saw in the previous chapter how many bytes each primitive type takes. Let's see how the memory consumption of the composite types looks with compressed pointers (a common case) on a 64-bit JVM with a heap size smaller than 32 GB:

Java Expression	64-bit memory usage	Description (b = bytes, padding toward memory word size in approximate multiples of 8)
`new Object()`	16 bytes	12 b header + 4 b padding
`new byte[0]`	16 bytes	12 b obj header + 4 b int length = 16 b array header
`new String("foo")`	40 bytes (interned for literals)	12 b header + (12 b array header + 6 b char-array content + 4 b length + 2 b padding = 24 b) + 4 b hash
`new Integer(3)`	16 bytes (boxed integer)	12 b header + 4 b int value
`new Long(4)`	24 bytes (boxed long)	12 b header + 8 b long value + 4 b padding
`class A { byte x; }` `new A();`	16 bytes	12 b header + 1 b value + 3 b padding

`class B extends A`
`{byte y;}`
`new B();`
	24 bytes (subclass padding)	12 b reference + (1 b value + 7 b padding = 8 b) for A + 1 b for value of y + 3 b padding

Java Expression	64-bit memory usage	Description (b = bytes, padding toward memory word size in approximate multiples of 8)

`clojure.lang.Symbol.intern("foo")`
 	
`// clojure 'foo`
	104 bytes (40 bytes interned)	12 b header + 12 b ns reference + (12 b name reference + 40 b interned chars) + 4 b int hash + 12 b meta reference + (12 b _str reference + 40 b interned chars) – 40 b interned `str`

`clojure.lang.Keyword.intern("foo")`
 	
`// clojure :foo`
	184 bytes (fully interned by factory method)	12 b reference + (12 b symbol reference + 104 b interned value) + 4 b int hash + (12 b _str reference + 40 b interned char)

A comparison of space taken by a symbol and a keyword created from the same given string demonstrates that even though a keyword has slight overhead over a symbol, the keyword is fully interned and would provide better guard against memory consumption and thus GC over time. Moreover, the keyword is interned as a weak reference, which ensures that it is garbage collected when no keyword in memory is pointing to the interned value anymore.

Determining program workload type

We often need to determine whether a program is CPU/cache bound, memory bound, I/O bound or contention bound. When a program is I/O or contention bound, the CPU usage is generally low. You may have to use a profiler (we will see this in *Chapter 7, Performance Optimization*) to find out whether threads are stuck due to resource contention. When a program is CPU/cache or memory bound, CPU usage may not be a clear indicator of the source of the bottleneck. In such cases, you may want to make an educated guess by inspecting cache misses in the program. On Linux systems tools such as **perf** (`https://perf.wiki.kernel.org/`), **cachegrind** (`http://valgrind.org/info/tools.html#cachegrind`) and **oprofile** (`http://oprofile.sourceforge.net/`) can help determine the volume of cache misses — a higher threshold may imply that the program is memory bound. However, using these tools with Java is not straightforward because Java's JIT compiler needs a warm-up until meaningful behavior can be observed. The project **perf-map-agent** (`https://github.com/jrudolph/perf-map-agent`) can help generate method mappings that you can correlate using the `perf` utility.

Tackling memory inefficiency

In earlier sections in this chapter we discussed that unchecked memory access may become a bottleneck. As of Java 8, due to the way the heap and object references work, we cannot fully control the object layout and memory access patterns. However, we can take care of the frequently executed blocks of code to consume less memory and attempt to make them cache-bound instead of memory-bound at runtime. We can consider a few techniques to lower memory consumption and randomness in access:

- Primitive locals (long, double, boolean, char, etc) in the JVM are created on the stack. The rest of the objects are created on the heap and only their references are stored in the stack. Primitives have a low overhead and do not require memory indirection for access, and are hence recommended.

- Data laid out in the main memory in a sequential fashion is faster to access than randomly laid out data. When we use a large (say more than eight elements) persistent map, the data stored in tries may not be sequentially laid out in memory, rather they would be randomly laid out in the heap. Moreover both keys and values are stored and accessed. When you use records (`defrecord`) and types (`deftype`), not only do they provide array/class semantics for the layout of fields within them, they do not store the keys, which is very efficient compared to regular maps.

- Reading large content from a disk or the network may have an adverse impact on performance due to random memory roundtrips. In *Chapter 3, Leaning on Java*, we briefly discussed memory-mapped byte buffers. You can leverage memory-mapped buffers to minimize fragmented object allocation/access on the heap. While libraries such as `nio` (`https://github.com/pjstadig/nio/`) and `clj-mmap` (`https://github.com/thebusby/clj-mmap`) help us deal with memory-mapped buffers, `bytebuffer` (`https://github.com/geoffsalmon/bytebuffer`), and `gloss` (`https://github.com/ztellman/gloss`) let us work with byte buffers. There are also alternate abstractions such as `iota` (`https://github.com/thebusby/iota`) that help us deal with large files as collections.

Given that memory bottleneck is a potential performance issue in data-intensive programs, lowering memory overhead goes a long way in avoiding performance risk. Understanding low-level details of the hardware, the JVM and Clojure's implementation helps us choose the appropriate techniques to tackle the memory bottleneck issue.

Measuring latency with Criterium

Clojure has a neat little macro called `time` that evaluates the body of code passed to it, and then prints out the time it took and simply returns the value. However, we can note that often the time taken to execute the code varies quite a bit across various runs:

```
user=> (time (reduce + (range 100000)))
"Elapsed time: 112.480752 msecs"
4999950000
user=> (time (reduce + (range 1000000)))
"Elapsed time: 387.974799 msecs"
499999500000
```

There are several reasons associated to this variance in behavior. When cold started, the JVM has its heap segments empty and is unaware of the code path. As the JVM keeps running, the heap fills up and the GC patterns start becoming noticeable. The JIT compiler gets a chance to profile the different code paths and optimize them. Only after quite some GC and JIT compilation rounds, does the JVM performance become less unpredictable.

Criterium (`https://github.com/hugoduncan/criterium`) is a Clojure library to scientifically measure the latency of Clojure expressions on a machine. A summary of how it works can be found at the Criterium project page. The easiest way to use Criterium is to use it with Leiningen. If you want Criterium to be available only in the REPL and not as a project dependency, add the following entry to the `~/.lein/profiles.clj` file:

```
{:user {:plugins [[criterium "0.4.3"]]}}
```

Another way is to include `criterium` in your project in the `project.clj` file:

```
:dependencies [[org.clojure/clojure "1.7.0"]
               [criterium "0.4.3"]]
```

Once done with the editing of the file, launch REPL using `lein repl`:

```
user=> (require '[criterium.core :as c])
nil
user=> (c/bench (reduce + (range 100000)))
Evaluation count : 1980 in 60 samples of 33 calls.
            Execution time mean : 31.627742 ms
    Execution time std-deviation : 431.917981 us
    Execution time lower quantile : 30.884211 ms ( 2.5%)
    Execution time upper quantile : 32.129534 ms (97.5%)
nil
```

Now, we can see that, on average, the expression took 31.6 ms on a certain test machine.

Criterium and Leiningen

By default, Leiningen starts the JVM in a low-tiered compilation mode, which causes it to start up faster but impacts the optimizations that the JRE can perform at runtime. To get the best effects when running tests with Criterium and Leiningen for a server-side use case, be sure to override the defaults in `project.clj` as follows:

```
:jvm-opts ^:replace ["-server"]
```

The `^:replace` hint causes Leiningen to replace its own defaults with what is provided under the `:jvm-opts` key. You may like to add more parameters as needed, such as a minimum and maximum heap size to run the tests.

Summary

The performance of a software system is directly impacted by its hardware components, so understanding how the hardware works is crucial. The processor, caches, memory, and I/O subsystems have different performance behaviors. Clojure, being a hosted language, understanding the performance properties of the host, that is, the JVM, is equally important. The Criterium library is useful for measuring the latency of the Clojure code—we will discuss Criterium again in *Chapter 6, Measuring Performance*. In the next chapter we will look at the concurrency primitives in Clojure and their performance characteristics.

5
Concurrency

Concurrency was one of the chief design goals of Clojure. Considering the concurrent programming model in Java (the comparison with Java is due to it being the predominant language on the JVM), it is not only too low level, but rather tricky to get right that without strictly following the patterns, one is more likely to shoot oneself in the foot. Locks, synchronization, and unguarded mutation are recipes for the concurrency pitfalls, unless exercised with extreme caution. Clojure's design choices deeply influence the way in which the concurrency patterns can be achieved in a safe and functional manner. In this chapter, we will discuss:

- The low level concurrency support at the hardware and JVM level
- The concurrency primitives of Clojure — atoms, agents, refs and vars
- The built-in concurrency that features in Java safe, and its usefulness with Clojure
- Parallelization with the Clojure features and reducers

Low-level concurrency

Concurrency cannot be achieved without explicit hardware support. We discussed about SMT and the multi-core processors in the previous chapters. Recall that every processor core has its own L1 cache, and several cores share the L2 cache. The shared L2 cache provides a fast mechanism to the processor cores to coordinate their cache access, eliminating the comparatively expensive memory access. Additionally, a processor buffers the writes to memory into something known as a **dirty write-buffer**. This helps the processor to issue a batch of memory update requests, reorder the instructions, and determine the final value to write to memory, known as **write absorption**.

Hardware memory barrier (fence) instructions

Memory access reordering is great for a sequential (single-threaded) program performance, but it is hazardous for the concurrent programs where the order of memory access in one thread may disrupt the expectations in another thread. The processor needs the means of synchronizing the access in such a way that memory reordering is either compartmentalized in code segments that do not care, or is prevented where it might have undesirable consequences. The hardware supports such a safety measure in terms of a "memory barrier" (also known as "fence").

There are several kinds of memory barrier instructions found in different architectures, with potentially different performance characteristics. The compiler (or the JIT compiler in the case of the JVM) usually knows about the fence instructions on the architectures that it runs on. The common fence instructions are read, write, acquire, and release barrier, and more. The barriers do not guarantee the latest data, rather they only control the relative ordering of memory access. Barriers cause the write-buffer to be flushed after all the writes are issued, before the barrier is visible to the processor that issued it.

Read and write barriers control the order of reads and writes respectively. Writes happen via a write-buffer; but reads may happen out of order, or from the write-buffer. To guarantee the correct ordering, acquire, and release, blocks/barriers are used. Acquire and release are considered "half barriers"; both of them together (acquire and release) form a "full barrier". A full barrier is more expensive than a half barrier.

Java support and the Clojure equivalent

In Java, the memory barrier instructions are inserted by the higher level coordination primitives. Even though fence instructions are expensive (hundreds of cycles) to run, they provide a safety net that makes accessing shared variables safe within the critical sections. In Java, the `synchronized` keyword marks a "critical section", which can be executed by only one thread at a time, thus making is a tool for "mutual exclusion". In Clojure, the equivalent of Java's `synchronized` is the `locking` macro:

```
// Java example
synchronized (someObject) {
    // do something
}
```

```
;; Clojure example
(locking some-object
   ;; do something
   )
```

The `locking` macro builds upon two special forms, `monitor-enter` and `monitor-exit`. Note that the `locking` macro is a low-level and imperative solution just like Java's `synchronized` – their use is not considered idiomatic Clojure. The special forms `monitor-enter` and `monitor-exit` respectively enter and exit the lock object's "monitor" – they are even lower level and not recommended for direct use.

Someone measuring the performance of the code that uses such locking should be aware of its single-threaded versus the multi-threaded latencies. Locking in a single thread is cheap. However, the performance penalty starts kicking in when there are two or more threads contending for a lock on the same object monitor. A lock is acquired on the monitor of an object called the "intrinsic" or "monitor" lock. Object equivalence (that is, when the = function returns as true) is never used for the purpose of locking. Make sure that the object references are the same (that is, when `identical?` returns as true) when locking from different threads.

Acquiring a monitor lock by a thread entails a read barrier, which invalidates the thread-local cached data, the corresponding processor registers, and the cache lines. This forces a reread from the memory. On the other hand, releasing the monitor lock results in a write barrier, which flushes all the changes to memory. These are expensive operations that impact parallelism, but they ensure consistency of data for all threads.

Java supports a `volatile` keyword for the data members in a class that guarantees read and write to an attribute outside of a synchronized block that would not be reordered. It is interesting to note that unless an attribute is declared `volatile`, it is not guaranteed to be visible in all the threads that are accessing it. The Clojure equivalent of Java's `volatile` is the metadata called `^:volatile-mutable` that we discussed in *Chapter 3, Leaning on Java*. An example of `volatile` in Java and Clojure is as follows:

```
// Java example
public class Person {
    volatile long age;
}
;; Clojure example
(deftype Person [^:volatile-mutable ^long age])
```

Reading and writing a `volatile` data requires read-acquire or write-release respectively, which means we need only a half-barrier to individually read or write the value. Note that due to a half-barrier, the read-followed-by-write operations are not guaranteed to be atomic. For example, the `age++` expression first reads the value, then increments and sets it. This makes two memory operations, which is no more a half-barrier.

Clojure 1.7 introduced a first class support for the volatile data using a new set of functions: `volatile!`, `vswap!`, `vreset!`, and `volatile?` These functions define volatile (mutable) data and work with that. However, make a note that these functions do not work with the volatile fields in `deftype`. You can see how to use them as follows:

```
user=> (def a (volatile! 10))
#'user/a
user=> (vswap! a inc)
11
user=> @a
11
user=> (vreset! a 20)
20
user=> (volatile? a)
true
```

Operations on volatile data are not atomic, which is why even creating a volatile (using `volatile!`) is considered potentially unsafe. In general, volatiles may be useful where read consistency is not a high priority but writes must be fast, such as real-time trend analysis, or other such analytics reporting. Volatiles may also be very useful when writing stateful transducers (refer to *Chapter 2, Clojure Abstractions*), serving as very fast state containers. In the next sub-section, we will see the other state abstractions that are safer (and mostly slower) than volatiles.

Atomic updates and state

It is a common use case to read a data element, execute some logic, and update with a new value. For single-threaded programs, it bears no consequences; but for concurrent scenarios, the entire operation must be carried out in a lockstep, as an atomic operation. This case is so common that many processors support this at the hardware level using a special Compare-and-swap (CAS) instruction, which is much cheaper than locking. On x86/x64 architectures, the instruction is called CompareExchange (CMPXCHG).

Unfortunately, it is possible that another thread updates the variable with the same value that the thread, which is working on the atomic update, is going to compare the old value against. This is known as the "ABA" problem. The set of instructions such as "Load-linked" (LL) and "Store-conditional" (SC), which are found in some other architectures, provide an alternative to CAS without the ABA problem. After the LL instruction reads the value from an address, the SC instruction to update the address with a new value will only go through if the address has not been updated since the LL instruction was successful.

Atomic updates in Java

Java has a bunch of built-in lock free, atomic, thread safe compare-and-swap abstractions for the state management. They live in the `java.util.concurrent.atomic` package. For primitive types, such as boolean, integer, and long, there are the `AtomicBoolean`, `AtomicInteger`, and `AtomicLong` classes respectively. The latter two classes support additional atomic add/subtract operations. For atomic reference updates, there are the `AtomicReference`, `AtomicMarkableReference`, and `AtomicStampedReference` classes for the arbitrary objects. There is also a support available for arrays where the array elements can be updated atomically — `AtomicIntegerArray`, `AtomicLongArray`, and `AtomicReferenceArray`. They are easy to use; here is the example:

```
(import 'java.util.concurrent.atomic.AtomicReference)
(def ^AtomicReference x (AtomicReference. "foo"))
(.compareAndSet x "foo" "bar")
(import 'java.util.concurrent.atomic.AtomicInteger)
(def ^AtomicInteger y (AtomicInteger. 10))
(.getAndAdd y 5)
```

However, where and how to use it is subjected to the update points and the logic in the code. The atomic updates are not guaranteed to be non-blocking. Atomic updates are not a substitute to locking in Java, but rather a convenience, only when the scope is limited to a compare and swap operation for one mutable variable.

Clojure's support for atomic updates

Clojure's atomic update abstraction is called "atom". It uses `AtomicReference` under the hood. An operation on `AtomicInteger` or `AtomicLong` may be slightly faster than on the Clojure `atom`, because the former uses primitives. But neither of them are too cheap, due to the compare-and-swap instruction that they use in the CPU. The speed really depends on how frequently the mutation happens, and how the JIT compiler optimizes the code. The benefit of speed may not show up until the code is run several hundred thousand times, and having an atom mutated very frequently will increase the latency due to the retries. Measuring the latency under actual (or similar to actual) load can tell better. An example of using an atom is as follows:

```
user=> (def a (atom 0))
#'user/a
user=> (swap! a inc)
1
user=> @a
1
user=> (compare-and-set! a 1 5)
true
user=> (reset! a 20)
20
```

The `swap!` function provides a notably different style of carrying out atomic updates than the `compareAndSwap(oldval, newval)` methods. While `compareAndSwap()` compares and sets the value, returning true if it's a success and false if it's a failure, `swap!` keeps on trying to update in an endless loop until it succeeds. This style is a popular pattern that is followed among Java developers. However, there is also a potential pitfall associated with the update-in-loop style. As the concurrency of the updaters gets higher, the performance of the update may gradually degrade. Then again, high concurrency on the atomic updates raises a question of whether or not uncoordinated updates was a good idea at all for the use-case. The `compare-and-set!` and `reset!` are pretty straightforward.

The function passed to `swap!` is required to be pure (as in side effect free), because it is retried several times in a loop during contention. If the function is not pure, the side effect may happen as many times as the retries.

It is noteworthy that atoms are not "coordinated", which means that when an atom is used concurrently by different threads, we cannot predict the order in which the operations work on it, and we cannot guarantee the end result as a consequence. The code we write around atoms should be designed with this constraint in mind. In many scenarios, atoms may not be a good fit due to the lack of coordination – watch out for that in the program design. Atoms support meta data and basic validation mechanism via extra arguments. The following examples illustrate these features:

```
user=> (def a (atom 0 :meta {:foo :bar}))
user=> (meta a)
{:foo :bar}
user=> (def age (atom 0 :validator (fn [x] (if (> x 200) false
true))))
user=> (reset! age 200)
200
user=> (swap! age inc)
IllegalStateException Invalid reference state  clojure.lang.ARef.
validate (ARef.java:33)
```

The second important thing is that atoms support is adding and removing watches on them. We will discuss watches later in the chapter.

Faster writes with atom striping

We know that atoms present contention when multiple threads try to update the state at the same time. This implies that atoms have great performance when the writes are infrequent. There are some use cases, for example metrics counters, where the writes need to be fast and frequent, but the reads are fewer and can tolerate some inconsistency. For such use cases, instead of directing all the updates to a single atom, we can maintain a bunch of atoms where each thread updates a different atom, thus reducing contention. Reads from these atoms cannot be guaranteed to be consistent. Let's develop an example of such a counter:

```
(def ^:const n-cpu (.availableProcessors (Runtime/getRuntime)))
(def counters (vec (repeatedly n-cpu #(atom 0))))
(defn inc! []
  ;; consider java.util.concurrent.ThreadLocalRandom in Java 7+
  ;; which is faster than Math/random that rand-int is based on
  (let [i (rand-int n-cpu)]
    (swap! (get counters i) inc)))
(defn value []
  (transduce (map deref) + counters))
```

In the previous example, we created a vector called counters of the same size as the number of CPU cores in the computer, and initialize each element with an atom of initial value 0. The function called inc! updates the counter by picking up a random atom from counters, and incrementing the value by 1. We also assumed that rand-int distributes the picking up of atom uniformly across all the processor cores, so that we have almost zero contention. The value function simply walks over all the atoms and adds up their deref'ed values to return the counter value. The example uses clojure.core/rand-int, which depends on java.lang.Math/random (due to Java 6 support) to randomly find out the next counter atom. Let's see how we can optimize this when using Java 7 or above:

```clojure
(import 'java.util.concurrent.ThreadLocalRandom)
(defn inc! []
  (let [i (.nextLong (ThreadLocalRandom/current) n-cpu)]
    (swap! (get counters i) inc)))
```

Here, we import the java.util.concurrent.ThreadLocalRandom class, and define the inc! function to pick up the next random atom using ThreadLocalRandom. Everything else remains the same.

Asynchronous agents and state

While atoms are synchronous, agents are the asynchronous mechanism in Clojure to effect any change in the state. Every agent is associated with a mutable state. We pass a function (known as "action") to an agent with the optional additional arguments. This function gets queued for processing in another thread by the agent. All the agents share two common thread pools—one for the low-latency (potentially CPU-bound, cache-bound, or memory-bound) jobs, and one for the blocking (potentially I/O related or lengthy processing) jobs. Clojure provides the send function for the low-latency actions, send-off for blocking actions, and send-via to have the action executed on the user-specified thread-pool, instead of either of the preconfigured thread pools. All of send, send-off, and send-via return immediately. Here is how we can use them:

```clojure
(def a (agent 0))
;; invoke (inc 0) in another thread and set state of a to result
(send a inc)
@a   ; returns 1
;; invoke (+ 1 2 3) in another thread and set state of a to result
(send a + 2 3)
```

```
@a   ; returns 6

(shutdown-agents)   ; shuts down the thread-pools
;; no execution of action anymore, hence no result update either
(send a inc)
@a   ; returns 6
```

When we inspect the Clojure (as of version 1.7.0) source code, we can find that the thread-pool for the low-latency actions is named as `pooledExecutor` (a bounded thread-pool, initialized to max '2 + number of hardware processors' threads), and the thread-pool for the high-latency actions is named as `soloExecutor` (an unbounded thread pool). The premise of this default configuration is that the CPU/cache/memory-bound actions run most optimally on a bounded thread-pool, with the default number of threads. The I/O bound tasks do not consume CPU resources. Hence, a relatively larger number of such tasks can execute at the same time, without significantly affecting the performance of the CPU/cache/memory-bound jobs. Here is how you can access and override the thread-pools:

```
(import 'clojure.lang.Agent)
Agent/pooledExecutor   ; thread-pool for low latency actions
Agent/soloExecutor   ; thread-pool for I/O actions
(import 'java.util.concurrent.Executors)
(def a-pool (Executors/newFixedThreadPool 10))   ; thread-pool with 10
threads
(def b-pool (Executors/newFixedThreadPool 100)) ; 100 threads pool
(def a (agent 0))
(send-via a-pool a inc)   ; use 'a-pool' for the action
(set-agent-send-executor! a-pool)   ; override default thread-pool
(set-agent-send-off-executor! b-pool)   ; override default pool
```

If a program carries out a large number of I/O or blocking operations through agents, it probably makes sense to limit the number of threads dedicated for such actions. Overriding the `send-off` thread-pool using `set-agent-send-off-executor!` is the easiest way to limit the thread-pool size. A more granular way to isolate and limit the I/O actions on the agents is to use `send-via` with the thread-pools of appropriate sizes for various kinds of I/O and blocking operations.

Asynchrony, queueing, and error handling

Sending an action to an agent returns immediately without blocking. If the agent is not already busy in executing any action, it "reacts" by enqueuing the action that triggers the execution of the action, in a thread, from the respective thread-pool. If the agent is busy in executing another action, the new action is simply enqueued. Once an action is executed from the action queue, the queue is checked for more entries and triggers the next action, if found. This whole "reactive" mechanism of triggering actions obviates the need of a message loop, polling the queue. This is only possible, because the entry points to an agent's queue are controlled.

Actions are executed asynchronously on agents, which raises the question of how the errors are handled. Error cases need to be handled with an explicit, predefined function. When using a default agent construction, such as (agent :foo), the agent is created without any error handler, and gets suspended in the event of any exception. It caches the exception, and refuses to accept any more actions. It throws the cached exception upon sending any action until the agent is restarted. A suspended agent can be reset using the restart-agent function. The objective of such suspension is safety and supervision. When the asynchronous actions are executed on an agent and suddenly an error occurs, it will require attention. Check out the following code:

```
(def g (agent 0))
(send g (partial / 10))  ; ArithmeticException due to divide-by-zero
@g  ; returns 0, because the error did not change the old state
(send g inc)  ; throws the cached ArithmeticException
(agent-error g)  ; returns (doesn't throw) the exception object
(restart-agent g @g)  ; clears the suspension of the agent
(agent-error g)  ; returns nil
(send g inc)  ; works now because we cleared the cached error
@g  ; returns 1
(dotimes [_ 1000] (send-off g long-task))
;; block for 100ms or until all actions over (whichever earlier)
(await-for 100 g)
(await g)  ; block until all actions dispatched till now are over
```

There are two optional parameters :error-handler and :error-mode, which we can configure on an agent to have finer control over the error handling and suspension as shown in the following code snippet:

```
(def g (agent 0 :error-handler (fn [x] (println "Found:" x))))  ;
incorrect arity
(send g (partial / 10))  ; no error encountered because error-handler
arity is wrong
```

```
(def g (agent 0 :error-handler (fn [ag x] (println "Found:" x))))  ;
correct arity
(send g (partial / 10))  ; prints the message
(set-error-handler! g (fn [ag x] (println "Found:" x)))  ; equiv of
:error-handler arg
(def h (agent 0 :error-mode :continue))
(send h (partial / 10))  ; error encountered, but agent not suspended
(send h inc)
@h  ; returns 1
(set-error-mode! h :continue)  ; equiv of :error-mode arg, other
possible value :fail
```

Why you should use agents

Just as the "atom" implementation uses only compare-and-swap instead of locking, the underlying "agent" specific implementation uses mostly the compare-and-swap operations. The agent implementation uses locks only when dispatching action in a transaction (discussed in the next section), or when restarting an agent. All the actions are queued and dispatched serially in the agents, regardless of the concurrency level. The serial nature makes it possible to execute the actions in an independent and contention-free manner. For the same agent, there can never be more than one action being executed. Since there is no locking, reads (deref or @) on agents are never blocked due to writes. However, all the actions are independent of each other — there is no overlap in their execution.

The implementation goes so far as to ensure that the execution of an action blocks other actions, which follow in the queue. Even though the actions are executed in a thread-pool, actions for the same agent are never executed concurrently. This is an excellent ordering guarantee that also extends a natural coordination mechanism, due to its serial nature. However, note that this ordering coordination is limited to only a single agent. If an agent action sends actions to two other agents, they are not automatically coordinated. In this situation, you may want to use transactions (which will be covered in the next section).

Since agents distinguish between the low-latency and blocking jobs, the jobs are executed in an appropriate kind of thread-pools. Actions on different agents may execute concurrently, thereby making optimum use of the threading resources. Unlike atoms, the performance of the agents is not impeded by high contention. In fact, for many cases, agents make a lot of sense due to the serial buffering of actions. In general, agents are great for high volume I/O tasks, or where the ordering of operations provides a win in the high contention scenarios.

Nesting

When an agent action sends another action to the same agent, that is a case of nesting. This would have been nothing special if agents didn't participate in STM transactions (which will be covered in the next section). However, agents do participate in STM transactions and that places certain constraints on agent implementation that warrants a second-layer buffering of actions. For now, it should suffice to say that the nested sends are queued in a thread-local queue instead of the regular queue in the agent. The thread-local queue is visible only to the thread in which the action is executed. Upon executing an action, unless there was an error, the agent implicitly calls the equivalent of `release-pending-sends` function, which transfers the actions from second level thread-local queue to the normal action queue. Note that nesting is simply an implementation detail of agents and has no other impact.

Coordinated transactional ref and state

We saw in an earlier section that an atom provides atomic read-and-update operation. What if we need to perform an atomic read-and-update operation across two or even more number of atoms? This clearly poses a coordination problem. Some entity has to watch over the process of reading and updating, so that the values are not corrupted. This is what a ref provides—a **Software Transactional Memory (STM)** based system that takes care of concurrent atomic read-and-update operations across multiple refs, such that either all the updates go through, or in the case of failure, none does. Like atoms, on failure, refs retry the whole operation from scratch with the new values.

Clojure's STM implementation is coarse grained. It works at the application level objects and aggregates (that is, references to aggregates), scoped to only all the refs in a program, constituting the "Ref world". Any update to a ref can only happen synchronously, in a transaction, in a `dosync` block of code, within the same thread. It cannot span beyond the current thread. The implementation detail reveals that a thread-local transaction context is maintained during a lifetime of a transaction. The same context ceases to be available, the moment the control reaches another thread.

Like the other reference types in Clojure, reads on a ref are never blocked by the updates, and vice versa. However, unlike the other reference types, the implementation of ref does not depend on a lock-free spinning, but rather, it internally uses locks, a low-level wait/notify, a deadlock detection, and the age-based barging.

The `alter` function is used to read-and-update the value of a ref, and `ref-set` is used to reset the value. Roughly, `alter` and `ref-set`, for the refs, are analogous to `swap!` and `reset!` for the atoms. Just like `swap!`, `alter` accepts a function (and arguments) with no side effects, and may be retried several times during the contention. However, unlike with the atoms, not only `alter` but also `ref-set` and simple `deref`, may cause a transaction to be retried during the contention. Here is a very simple example on how we may use a transaction:

```
(def r1 (ref [:a :b :c]))
(def r2 (ref [1 2 3]))
(alter r1 conj :d)   ; IllegalStateException No transaction running...
(dosync (let [v (last @r1)] (alter r1 pop) (alter r2 conj v)))
@r1   ; returns [:a :b]
@r2   ; returns [1 2 3 :c]
(dosync (ref-set r1 (conj @r1 (last @r2))) (ref-set r2 (pop @r2)))
@r1   ; returns [:a :b :c]
@r2   ; returns [1 2 3]
```

Ref characteristics

Clojure maintains the **Atomicity**, **Consistency**, and **Isolation** (**ACI**) characteristics in a transaction. This overlaps with A, C, and I of the ACID guarantee that many databases provide. Atomicity implies that either all of the updates in a transaction will complete successfully or none of them do. Consistency means that the transaction must maintain general correctness, and should honor the constraints set by the validation—any exception or validation error should roll back the transaction. Unless a shared state is guarded, concurrent updates on it may lead a multi-step transaction into seeing different values at different steps. Isolation implies that all the steps in a transaction will see the same value, no matter how concurrent the updates are.

The Clojure refs use something known as **Multi Version Concurrency Control** (**MVCC**) to provide **Snapshot Isolation** to the transactions. In MVCC, instead of locking (which could block the transactions), the queues are maintained, so that each transaction can occur using its own snapshot copy, taken at its "read point", independent of other transactions. The main benefit of this approach is that the read-only out-of-transaction operations can go through without any contention. Transactions without the ref contention go through concurrently. In a rough comparison with the database systems, the Clojure ref isolation level is "Read Committed" for reading a Ref outside of a transaction, and "Repeatable Read" by default when inside the transaction.

Ref history and in-transaction deref operations

We discussed earlier that both, read and update operations, on a ref, may cause a transaction to be retried. The reads in a transaction can be configured to use the ref history in such a manner that the snapshot isolation instances are stored in the history queues, and are used by the read operations in the transactions. The default, which is not supposed to use the history queues, conserves heap space, and provides strong consistency (avoids the staleness of data) in the transactions.

Using the ref history reduces the likelihood of the transaction retries caused by read contention, thereby providing a weak consistency. Therefore, it is a tool for performance optimization, which comes at the cost of consistency. In many scenarios, programs do not need strong consistency — we can choose appropriately if we know the trade-off, and what we need. The snapshot isolation mechanism in the Clojure ref implementation is backed by the adaptive history queues. The history queues grow dynamically to meet the read requests, and do not overshoot the maximum limit that is set for the ref. By default, the history is not enabled, so we need to specify it during the initialization or set it later. Here is an example of how to use the history:

```
(def r (ref 0 :min-history 5 :max-history 10))
(ref-history-count r)   ; returns 0, because no snapshot instances are
queued so far
(ref-min-history r)   ; returns 5
(ref-max-history r)   ; returns 10
(future (dosync (println "Sleeping 20 sec") (Thread/sleep 20000) (ref-
set r 10)))
(dosync (alter r inc))   ; enter this within few seconds after the
previous expression
;; The message "Sleeping 20 sec" should appear twice due to
transaction-retry
(ref-history-count r)   ; returns 2, the number of snapshot history
elements
(.trimHistory ^clojure.lang.Ref r)
(ref-history-count r)   ; returns 0 because we wiped the history
(ref-min-history r 10)   ; reset the min history
(ref-max-history r 20)   ; reset the max history count
```

Minimum/maximum history limits are proportional to the length of the staleness window of the data. It also depends on the relative latency difference of the update and read operations to see what the range of the min-history and the max-history works well on a given host system. It may take some amount of trial and error to get the range right. As a ballpark figure, read operations only need as many min-history elements to avoid the transaction retries, as many updates can go through during one read operation. The max-history elements can be a multiple of min-history to cover for any history overrun or underrun. If the relative latency difference is unpredictable, then we have to either plan a min-history for the worst case scenario, or consider other approaches.

Transaction retries and barging

A transaction can internally be in one of the five distinct states—Running, Committing, Retry, Killed, and Committed. A transaction can be killed for various reasons. Exceptions are the common reasons for killing a transaction. But let's consider the corner case where a transaction is retried many times, but it does not appear to commit successfully—what is the resolution? Clojure supports age-based barging, wherein an older transaction automatically tries to abort a younger transaction, so that the younger transaction is retried later. If the barging still doesn't work, as a last resort, the transaction is killed after a hard limit of 10,000 retry attempts, and then the exception is thrown.

Upping transaction consistency with ensure

Clojure's transactional consistency is a good balance between performance and safety. However, at times, we may need the **Serializable** consistency in order to preserve the correctness of the transaction. Concretely, in the face of the transaction retries, when a transaction's correctness depends on the state of a ref, in the transaction, wherein the ref is updated simultaneously in another transaction, we have a condition called "write skew". The Wikipedia entry on the write skew, `https://en.wikipedia.org/wiki/Snapshot_isolation`, describes it well, but let's see a more concrete example. Let's say we want to design a flight simulation system with two engines, and one of the system level constraints is not to switch off both engines at the same time. If we model each engine as a ref, and certain maneuvers do require us to switch off an engine, we must ensure that the other engine is on. We can do it with `ensure`. Usually, `ensure` is required when maintaining a consistent relationship (invariants) across the refs is necessary. This cannot be ensured by the validator functions, because they do not come into play until the transaction commits. The validator functions will see the same value hence cannot help.

The write-skew can be solved using the namesake `ensure` function that essentially prevents a ref from modification by other transactions. It is similar to a locking operation, but in practice, it provides better concurrency than the explicit read-and-update operations, when the retries are expensive. Using `ensure` is quite simple— `(ensure ref-object)`. However, it may be performance-wise expensive, due to the locks it holds during the transaction. Managing performance with `ensure` involves a trade-off between the retry latency, and the lost throughput due to the ensured state.

Lesser transaction retries with commutative operations

Commutative operations are independent of the order in which they are applied. For example, incrementing a counter ref c1 from transactions t1 and t2 would have the same effect irrespective of the order in which t1 and t2 commit their changes. Refs have a special optimization for changing functions that are commutative for transactions—the `commute` function, which is similar to `alter` (same syntax), but with different semantics. Like `alter`, the `commute` functions are applied atomically during the transaction commit. However, unlike `alter`, `commute` does not cause the transaction retry on contention, and there is no guarantee about the order in which the `commute` functions are applied. This effectively makes `commute` nearly useless for returning a meaningful value as a result of the operation. All the commute functions in a transaction are reapplied with the final in transaction ref values during the transaction commit.

As we can see, commute reduces the contention, thereby optimizing the performance of the overall transaction throughput. Once we know that an operation is commutative and we are not going to use its return value in a meaningful way, there is hardly any trade-off deciding on whether to use it—we should just go ahead and use it. In fact, a program design, with respect to the ref transactions, with commute in mind, is not a bad idea.

Agents can participate in transactions

In the previous section on agents, we discussed how agents work with the queued change functions. Agents can also participate in the ref transactions, thereby making it possible to combine the use of refs and agents in the transactions. However, agents are not included in the "Ref world", hence a transaction scope is not extended till the execution of the change function in an agent. Rather, the transactions only make sure that the changes sent to the agents are queued until the transaction commit happens.

The *Nesting* sub-section, in the earlier section on agents, discusses about a second-layer thread-local queue. This thread-local queue is used during a transaction to hold the sent changes to an agent until the commit. The thread-local queue does not block the other changes that are being sent to an agent. The out-of-transaction changes are never buffered in the thread-local queue; rather, they are added to the regular queue in the agent.

The participation of agents in the transactions provides an interesting angle of design, where the coordinated and independent/sequential operations can be pipelined as a workflow for better throughput and performance.

Nested transactions

Clojure transactions are nesting aware and they compose well. But, why would one need a nested transaction? Often, independent units of code may have their own low-granularity transactions that a higher level code can make use of. When the higher level caller itself needs to wrap actions in a transaction, nested transactions occur. Nested transactions have their own lifecycle and run-state. However, an outer transaction can abort an inner transaction on the detection of failure.

The "ref world" snapshot `ensures` and `commutes` are shared among all (that is, outer and inner) levels of a nested transaction. Due to this, the inner transaction is treated as any other ref change operation (similar to `alter`, `ref-set` and so on) within an outer transaction. The watches and internal lock implementation are handled at the respective nesting level. The detection of contention in the inner transactions causes a restart of not only the inner but also the outer transaction. Commits at all the levels are effected as a global state finally when the outermost transaction commits. The watches, even though tracked at each individual transaction level, are finally effected during the commit. A closer look at the nested transaction implementation shows that nesting has little or no impact on the performance of transactions.

Performance considerations

Clojure Ref is likely to be the most complex reference type implemented yet. Due to its characteristics, especially its transaction retry mechanism, it may not be immediately apparent that such a system would have good performance during the high-contention scenarios.

Understanding its nuances and best ways of use should help:

- We do not use changes with the side effects in a transaction, except for possibly sending the I/O changes to agents, where the changes are buffered until the commit. So by definition, we do not carry out any expensive I/O work in a transaction. Hence, a retry of this work would be cheap as well.

- A change function for a transaction should be as small as possible. This lowers the latency and hence, the retries will also be cheaper.

- Any ref that is not updated along with at least one more ref simultaneously needs not be a ref—atoms would do just fine in this case. Now that the refs make sense only in a group, their contention is directly proportional to the group size. Small groups of refs used in the transactions lead to a low contention, lower latency, and a higher throughput.

- Commutative functions provide a good opportunity to enhance the transaction throughput without any penalty. Identifying such cases and designing with commute in mind can help performance significantly.

- Refs are very coarse grained—they work at the application aggregate level. Often a program may need to have more fine-grained control over the transaction resources. This can be enabled by Ref striping, such as Megaref (`https://github.com/cgrand/megaref`), by providing a scoped view on the associative refs, thereby allowing higher concurrency.

- In the high contention scenarios in which the ref group size in a transaction cannot be small, consider using agents, as they have no contention due to the serial nature. Agents may not be a replacement for the transactions, but rather we can employ a pipeline consisting of atoms, refs, and agents to ease out the contention versus latency concerns.

Refs and transactions have an intricate implementation. Fortunately, we can inspect the source code, and browse through available online and offline resources.

Dynamic var binding and state

The fourth kind among the Clojure's reference types is the dynamic var. Since Clojure 1.3, all the vars are static by default. A var must be explicitly declared so in order to be dynamic. Once declared, a dynamic var can be bound to new values on per-thread basis. Binding on different threads do not block each other. An example is shown here:

```
(def ^:dynamic *foo* "bar")
(println *foo*)   ; prints bar
```

```
(binding [*foo* "baz"] (println *foo*))  ; prints baz
(binding [*foo* "bar"] (set! *foo* "quux") (println *foo*))  ; prints
quux
```

As the dynamic binding is thread-local, it may be tricky to use in multi-threaded scenarios. Dynamic vars have been long abused by libraries and applications as a means to pass in a common argument to be used by several functions. However, this style is acknowledged to be an anti-pattern, and is discouraged. Typically, in the anti-pattern dynamic, vars are wrapped by a macro to contain the dynamic thread-local binding in the lexical scope. This causes problems with the multi-threading and lazy sequences.

So, how can the dynamic vars be used effectively? A dynamic var lookup is more expensive than looking up a static var. Even passing a function argument is performance-wise much cheaper than looking up a dynamic var. Binding a dynamic var incurs additional cost. Clearly, in performance sensitive code, dynamic vars are best not used at all. However, dynamic vars may prove to be useful to hold a temporary thread-local state in a complex, or recursive call-graph scenario, where the performance does not matter significantly, without being advertised or leaked into the public API. The dynamic var bindings can nest and unwind like a stack, which makes them both attractive and suitable for such tasks.

Validating and watching the reference types

Vars (both static and dynamic), atoms, refs, and agents provide a way to validate the value being set as state—a `validator` function that accepts new value as argument, and returns the logical as true if it succeeds, or throws exception/returns logical as false (the false and nil values) if there's an error. They all honor what the validator function returns. If it is a success, the update goes through, and if an error, an exception is thrown instead. Here is the syntax on how the validators can be declared and associated with the reference types:

```
(def t (atom 1 :validator pos?))
(def g (agent 1 :validator pos?))
(def r (ref 1 :validator pos?))
(swap! t inc)  ; goes through, because value after increment (2) is
positive
(swap! t (constantly -3))  ; throws exception
(def v 10)
```

```
(set-validator! (var v) pos?)
(set-validator! t (partial < 10)) ; throws exception
(set-validator! g (partial < 10)) ; throws exception
(set-validator! r #(< % 10)) ; works
```

Validators cause actual failure within a reference type while updating them. For vars and atoms, they simply prevent the update by throwing an exception. In an agent, a validation failure causes agent failure, and needs the agent to restart. Inside a ref, the validation failure causes the transaction to rollback and rethrow the exception.

Another mechanism to observe the changes to the reference types is a "watcher". Unlike validators, a watcher is passive — it is notified of the update after the fact. Hence, a watcher cannot prevent updates from going through, because it is only a notification mechanism. For transactions, a watcher is invoked only after the transaction commit. While only one validator can be set on a reference type, it is possible to associate multiple watchers to a reference type on the other hand. Secondly, when adding a watch, we can specify a key, so that the notifications can be identified by the key, and be dealt accordingly by the watcher. Here is the syntax on how to use watchers:

```
(def t (atom 1))
(defn w [key iref oldv newv] (println "Key:" key "Old:" oldv "New:"
newv))
(add-watch t :foo w)
(swap! t inc)  ; prints "Key: :foo Old: 1 New: 2"
```

Like validators, the watchers are executed synchronously in the thread of the reference type. For atoms and refs, this may be fine, since the notification to the watchers goes on, the other threads may proceed with their updates. However in agents, the notification happens in the same thread where the update happens — this makes the update latency higher, and the throughput potentially lower.

Java concurrent data structures

Java has a number of mutable data structures that are meant for concurrency and thread-safety, which implies that multiple callers can safely access these data structures at the same time, without blocking each other. When we need only the highly concurrent access without the state management, these data structures may be a very good fit. Several of these employ lock free algorithms. We discussed about the Java atomic state classes in the *Atomic updates and state section*, so we will not repeat them here. Rather, we will only discuss the concurrent queues and other collections.

All of these data structures live in the `java.util.concurrent` package. These concurrent data structures are tailored to leverage the JSR 133 "Java Memory Model and Thread Specification Revision" (`http://gee.cs.oswego.edu/dl/jmm/cookbook.html`) implementation that first appeared in Java 5.

Concurrent maps

Java has a mutable concurrent hash map — `java.util.concurrent.ConcurrentHashMap` (CHM in short). The concurrency level can be optionally specified when instantiating the class, which is 16 by default. The CHM implementation internally partitions the map entries into the hash buckets, and uses multiple locks to reduce the contention on each bucket. Reads are never blocked by writes, therefore they may be stale or inconsistent — this is countered by built-in detection of such situations, and issuing a lock in order to read the data again in the synchronized fashion. This is an optimization for the scenarios, where reads significantly outnumber writes. In CHM, all the individual operations are near constant-time unless stuck in a retry loop due to the lock contention.

In contrast with Clojure's persistent map, CHM cannot accept `null` (`nil`) as the key or value. Clojure's immutable scalars and collections are automatically well-suited for use with CHM. An important thing to note is that only the individual operations in CHM are atomic, and exhibit strong consistency. As CHM operations are concurrent, the aggregate operations provide a rather weak consistency than the true operation-level consistency. Here is how we can use CHM. The individual operations in CHM, which provide a better consistency, are safe to use. The aggregate operations should be reserved for when we know its consistency characteristics, and the related trade-off:

```
(import 'java.util.concurrent.ConcurrentHashMap)
(def ^ConcurrentHashMap m (ConcurrentHashMap.))
(.put m :english "hi")                    ; individual operation
(.get m :english)                         ; individual operation
(.putIfAbsent m :spanish "alo")     ; individual operation
(.replace m :spanish "hola")          ; individual operation
(.replace m :english "hi" "hello")  ; individual compare-and-swap
atomic operation
(.remove m :english)                      ; individual operation
(.clear m)      ; aggregate operation
(.size m)        ; aggregate operation
(count m)      ; internally uses the .size() method
;; aggregate operation
```

```
(.putAll m {:french "bonjour" :italian "buon giorno"})
(.keySet m)    ; aggregate operation
(keys m)       ; calls CHM.entrySet() and on each pair java.util.Map.
Entry.getKey()
(vals m)       ; calls CHM.entrySet() and on each pair java.util.Map.
Entry.getValue()
```

The `java.util.concurrent.ConcurrentSkipListMap` class (CSLM in short) is another concurrent mutable map data structure in Java. The difference between CHM and CSLM is that CSLM offers a sorted view of the map at all times with the O(log N) time complexity. The sorted view has the natural order of keys by default, which can be overridden by specifying a Comparator implementation when instantiating CSLM. The implementation of CSLM is based on the Skip List, and provides navigation operations.

The `java.util.concurrent.ConcurrentSkipListSet` class (CSLS in short) is a concurrent mutable set based on the CSLM implementation. While CSLM offers the map API, CSLS behaves as a set data structure while borrowing features of CSLM.

Concurrent queues

Java has a built-in implementation of several kinds of mutable and concurrent in-memory queues. The queue data structure is a useful tool for buffering, producer-consumer style implementation, and for pipelining such units together to form the high-performance workflows. We should not confuse them with durable queues that are used for similar purpose in the batch jobs for a high throughput. Java's in-memory queues are not transactional, but they provide atomicity and strong consistency guarantee for the individual queue operations only. Aggregate operations offer weaker consistency.

The `java.util.concurrent.ConcurrentLinkedQueue` (CLQ) is a lock-free, wait-free unbounded "First In First Out" (FIFO) queue. FIFO implies that the order of the queue elements will not change once added to the queue. CLQ's `size()` method is not a constant time operation; it depends on the concurrency level. Few examples of using CLQ are here:

```
(import 'java.util.concurrent.ConcurrentLinkedQueue)
(def ^ConcurrentLinkedQueue q (ConcurrentLinkedQueue.))
(.add q :foo)
(.add q :bar)
(.poll q)   ; returns :foo
(.poll q)   ; returns :bar
```

Queue	Blocking?	Bounded?	FIFO?	Fairness?	Notes
CLQ	No	No	Yes	No	Wait-free, but the size() is not constant time
ABQ	Yes	Yes	Yes	Optional	The capacity is fixed at instantiation
DQ	Yes	No	No	No	The elements implement the Delayed interface
LBQ	Yes	Optional	Yes	No	The capacity is flexible, but with no fairness option
PBQ	Yes	No	No	No	The elements are consumed in a priority order
SQ	Yes	–	–	Optional	It has no capacity; it serves as a channel

In the `java.util.concurrent` package, `ArrayBlockingQueue` (ABQ), `DelayQueue` (DQ), `LinkedBlockingQueue` (LBQ), `PriorityBlockingQueue` (PBQ), and `SynchronousQueue` (SQ) implement the `BlockingQueue` (BQ) interface. Its Javadoc describes the characteristics of its method calls. ABQ is a fixed-capacity, FIFO queue backed by an array. LBQ is also a FIFO queue, backed by the linked nodes, and is optionally bounded (default `Integer.MAX_VALUE`). ABQ and LBQ generate "Back pressure" by blocking the enqueue operations on full capacity. ABQ supports optional fairness (with performance overhead) in the order of the threads that access it.

DQ is an unbounded queue that accepts the elements associated with the delay. The queue elements cannot be null, and must implement the `java.util. concurrent.Delayed` interface. Elements are available for removal from the queue only after the delay has been expired. DQ can be very useful for scheduling the processing of the elements at different times.

PBQ is unbounded and blocking while letting elements be consumed from the queue as per priority. Elements have the natural ordering by default that can be overridden by specifying a Comparator implementation when instantiating the queue.

SQ is not really a queue at all. Rather, it's just a barrier for a producer or consumer thread. The producer blocks until a consumer removes the element and vice versa. SQ does not have a capacity. However, SQ supports optional fairness (with performance overhead), in the order, in which the threads access it.

There are some new concurrent queue types introduced after Java 5. Since JDK 1.6, in the `java.util.concurrent` package Java has **BlockingDeque (BD)** with **LinkedBlockingDeque (LBD)** as the only available implementation. BD builds on BQ by adding the **Deque (double-ended queue)** operations, that is, the ability to add elements and consume the elements from both the ends of the queue. LBD can be instantiated with an optional capacity (bounded) to block the overflow. JDK 1.7 introduced **TransferQueue (TQ)** with **LinkedTransferQueue (LTQ)** as the only implementation. TQ extends the concept of SQ in such a way that the producers and consumers block a queue of elements. This will help utilize the producer and consumer threads better by keeping them busy. LTQ is an unbounded implementation of TQ where the `size()` method is not a constant time operation.

Clojure support for concurrent queues

We covered the persistent queue in *Chapter 2, Clojure Abstractions* earlier. Clojure has a built-in `seque` function that builds over a BQ implementation (LBQ by default) to expose a write-ahead sequence. The sequence is potentially lazy, and the write-ahead buffer throttles how many elements to realize. As opposed to the chunked sequences (of chunk size 32), the size of the write-ahead buffer is controllable and potentially populated at all times until the source sequence is exhausted. Unlike the chunked sequences, the realization doesn't happen suddenly for a chunk of 32 elements. It does so gradually and smoothly.

Under the hood, Clojure's `seque` uses an agent to the backfill data in the write-ahead buffer. In the arity-2 variant of `seque`, the first argument should either be a positive integer, or an instance of BQ (ABQ, LBQ, and more) that is preferably bounded.

Concurrency with threads

On the JVM, threads are the de-facto fundamental instrument of concurrency. Multiple threads live in the same JVM; they share the heap space, and compete for the resources.

JVM support for threads

The JVM threads are the Operating System threads. Java wraps an underlying OS thread as an instance of the `java.lang.Thread` class, and builds up an API around it to work with threads. A thread on the JVM has a number of states: New, Runnable, Blocked, Waiting, Timed_Waiting, and Terminated. A thread is instantiated by overriding the `run()` method of the `Thread` class, or by passing an instance of the `java.lang.Runnable` interface to the constructor of the `Thread` class.

Invoking the `start()` method of a `Thread` instance starts its execution in a new thread. Even if just a single thread runs in the JVM, the JVM would not shut down. Calling the `setDaemon(boolean)` method of a thread with argument `true` tags the thread as a daemon that can be automatically shut down if no other non-daemon thread is running.

All Clojure functions implement the `java.lang.Runnable` interface. Therefore, invoking a function in a new thread is very easy:

```
(defn foo5 [] (dotimes [_ 5] (println "Foo")))
(defn barN [n] (dotimes [_ n] (println "Bar")))
(.start (Thread. foo5))   ; prints "Foo" 5 times
(.start (Thread. (partial barN 3)))   ; prints "Bar" 3 times
```

The `run()` method does not accept any argument. We can work around it by creating a higher order function that needs no arguments, but internally applies the argument `3`.

Thread pools in the JVM

Creating threads leads to the Operating System API calls, which is not always a cheap operation. The general practice is to create a pool of threads that can be recycled for different tasks. Java has a built-in support for threads pools. The interface called `java.util.concurrent.ExecutorService` represents the API for a thread pool. The most common way to create a thread pool is to use a factory method in the `java.util.concurrent.Executors` class:

```
(import 'java.util.concurrent.Executors)
(import 'java.util.concurrent.ExecutorService)
(def ^ExecutorService a (Executors/newSingleThreadExecutor))   ;
bounded pool
(def ^ExecutorService b (Executors/newCachedThreadPool))   ; unbounded
pool
(def ^ExecutorService c (Executors/newFixedThreadPool 5))   ; bounded
pool
(.execute b #(dotimes [_ 5] (println "Foo")))   ; prints "Foo" 5 times
```

The previous example is equivalent of the examples with raw threads that we saw in the previous sub-section. Thread pools are also capable of helping to track the completion, and the return value of a function, executed in a new thread. An ExecutorService accepts an instance of the `java.util.concurrent.Callable` instance as an argument to several methods that launch a task, and return `java.util.concurrent.Future` to track the final result.

All the Clojure functions also implement the `Callable` interface, so we can use them as follows:

```
(import 'java.util.concurrent.Callable)
(import 'java.util.concurrent.Future)
(def ^ExecutorService e (Executors/newSingleThreadExecutor))
(def ^Future f (.submit e (cast Callable #(reduce + (range
10000000)))))
(.get f)  ; blocks until result is processed, then returns it
```

The thread pools described here are the same as the ones that we saw briefly in the Agents section earlier. Thread pools need to be shut down by calling the `shutdown()` method when no longer required.

Clojure concurrency support

Clojure has some nifty built-in features to deal with concurrency. We already discussed about the agents, and how they use the thread pools, in an earlier section. There are some more concurrency features in Clojure to deal with the various use cases.

Future

We saw earlier in this section how to use the Java API to launch a new thread, to execute a function. Also, we learned how to get the result back. Clojure has a built-in support called "futures" to do these things in a much smoother and integrated manner. The basis of the futures is the function `future-call` (it takes a `no-arg` function as an argument), and the macro `future` (it takes the body of code) that builds on the former. Both of them immediately start a thread to execute the supplied code. The following snippet illustrates the functions that work with the future, and how to use them:

```
;; runs body in new thread
(def f (future (println "Calculating") (reduce + (range 1e7))))
(def g (future-call #(do (println "Calculating") (reduce + (range
1e7)))))  ; takes no-arg fn
(future? f)                      ; returns true
(future-cancel g)          ; cancels execution unless already over (can
stop mid-way)
(future-cancelled? g) ; returns true if canceled due to request
```

```
(future-done? f)            ; returns true if terminated successfully, or
canceled
(realized? f)               ; same as future-done? for futures
@f                          ; blocks if computation not yet over
(use deref for timeout)
```

One of the interesting aspects of future-cancel is that it can sometimes not only cancel tasks that haven't started yet, but may also abort those that are halfway through execution:

```
(let [f (future (println "[f] Before sleep")
                (Thread/sleep 2000)
                (println "[f] After sleep")
                2000)]
  (Thread/sleep 1000)
  (future-cancel f)
  (future-cancelled? f))
;; [f] Before sleep  ← printed message (second message is never
printed)
;; true  ← returned value (due to future-cancelled?)
```

The previous scenario happens because Clojure's future-cancel cancels a future in such a way that if the execution has already started, it may be interrupted causing InterruptedException, which, if not explicitly caught, would simply abort the block of code. Beware of exceptions arising from the code that is executed in a future, because, by default, they are not reported verbosely! Clojure futures use the "solo" thread pool (used to execute the potentially blocking actions) that we discussed earlier with respect to the agents.

Promise

A promise is a placeholder for the result of a computation that may or may not have occurred. A promise is not directly associated with any computation. By definition, a promise does not imply when the computation might occur, hence realizing the promise.

Typically, a promise originates from one place in the code, and is realized by some other portion of the code that knows when and how to realize the promise. Very often, this happens in a multi-threaded code. If a promise is not realized yet, any attempt to read the value blocks all callers. If a promise is realized, then all the callers can read the value without being blocked. As with futures, a promise can be read with a timeout using deref.

Here is a very simple example showing how to use promises:

```
(def p (promise))
(realized? p)  ; returns false
@p  ; at this point, this will block until another thread delivers the
promise
(deliver p :foo)
@p  ; returns :foo (for timeout use deref)
```

A promise is a very powerful tool that can be passed around as function arguments. It can be stored in a reference type, or simply be used for a high level coordination.

Clojure parallelization and the JVM

We observed in *Chapter 1, Performance by Design* that parallelism is a function of the hardware, whereas concurrency is a function of the software, assisted by the hardware support. Except for the algorithms that are purely sequential by nature, concurrency is the favored means to facilitate parallelism, and achieve better performance. Immutable and stateless data is a catalyst to concurrency, as there is no contention between threads, due to absence of mutable data.

Moore's law

In 1965, Intel's cofounder, Gordon Moore, made an observation that the number of transistors per square inch on Integrated Circuits doubles every 24 months. He also predicted that the trend would continue for 10 years, but in practice, it has continued till now, marking almost half a century. More transistors have resulted in more computing power. With a greater number of transistors in the same area, we need higher clock speed to transmit signals to all of the transistors. Secondly, transistors need to get smaller in size to fit in. Around 2006-2007, the clock speed that the circuitry could work with topped out at about 2.8GHz, due to the heating issues and the laws of physics. Then, the multi-core processors were born.

Amdahl's law

The multi-core processors naturally require splitting up computation in order to achieve parallelization. Here begins a conflict—a program that was made to be run sequentially cannot make use of the parallelization features of the multi-core processors. The program must be altered to find the opportunity to split up computation at every step, while keeping the cost of coordination in mind. This results in a limitation that a program can be no more faster than its longest sequential part (*contention*, or *seriality*), and the coordination overhead. This characteristic was described by Amdahl's law.

Universal Scalability Law

Dr Neil Gunther's Universal Scalability Law (USL) is a superset of Amdahl's Law that makes both: *contention (a)* and *coherency (β)* the first class concerns in quantifying the scalability very closely to the realistic parallel systems. Coherency implies the coordination overhead (latency) in making the result of one part of a parallelized program to be available to another. While Amdahl's Law states that contention (seriality) causes performance to level off, USL goes to show that the performance actually degrades with excessive parallelization. USL is described with the following formula:

$$C(N) = N / (1 + α ((N - 1) + β N (N - 1)))$$

Here, C(N) implies relative capacity or throughput in terms of the source of concurrency, such as physical processors, or the users driving the software application. α implies the degree of contention because of the shared data or the sequential code, and β implies penalty incurred for maintaining the consistency of shared data. I would encourage you to pursue USL further (`http://www.perfdynamics.com/Manifesto/USLscalability.html`), as this is a very important resource for studying the impact of concurrency on scalability and the performance of the systems.

Clojure support for parallelization

A program that relies on mutation cannot parallelize its parts without creating contention on the mutable state. It requires coordination overhead, which makes the situation worse. Clojure's immutable nature is better suited to parallelize the parts of a program. Clojure also has some constructs that are suited for parallelism by the virtue of Clojure's consideration of available hardware resources. The result is, the operations execute optimized for certain use case scenarios.

pmap

The `pmap` function (similar to `map`) accepts as arguments a function and one, or more collections of data elements. The function is applied to each of the data elements in such a way that some of the elements are processed by the function in parallel. The parallelism factor is chosen at runtime by the `pmap` implementation, as two greater than the total number of available processors. It still processes the elements lazily, but the realization factor is same as the parallelism factor.

Check out the following code:

```
(pmap (partial reduce +)
       [(range 1000000)
        (range 1000001 2000000)
        (range 2000001 3000000)])
```

To use `pmap` effectively, it is imperative that we understand what it is meant for. As the documentation says, it is meant for computationally intensive functions. It is optimized for CPU-bound and cache-bound jobs. High latency and low CPU tasks, such as blocking I/O, are a gross misfit for `pmap`. Another pitfall to be aware of is whether the function used in `pmap` performs a lot of memory operations or not. Since the same function will be applied across all the threads, all the processors (or cores) may compete for the memory interconnect and the sub-system bandwidth. If the parallel memory access becomes a bottleneck, `pmap` cannot make the operation truly parallel, due to the contention on the memory access.

Another concern is what happens when several `pmap` operations run concurrently? Clojure does not attempt to detect multiple `pmaps` running concurrently. The same number of threads will be launched afresh for every new `pmap` operation. The developer is responsible to ensure the performance characteristics, and the response time of the program resulting from the concurrent pmap executions. Usually, when the latency reasons are paramount, it is advisable to limit the concurrent instances of `pmap` running in the program.

pcalls

The `pcalls` function is built using `pmap`, so it borrows properties from the latter. However, the `pcalls` function accepts zero or more functions as arguments and executes them in parallel, returning the result values of the calls as a list.

pvalues

The `pvalues` macro is built using `pcalls`, so it transitively shares the properties of `pmap`. It's behavior is similar to `pcalls`, but instead of functions, it accepts zero or more S-expressions that are evaluated in the parallel using `pmap`.

Java 7's fork/join framework

Java 7 introduced a new framework for parallelism called "fork/join," based on divide-and-conquer and the work-stealing scheduler algorithms. The basic idea of how to use the fork/join framework is fairly simple—if the work is small enough, then do it directly in the same thread; otherwise, split the work into two pieces, invoke them in a fork/join thread pool, and wait for the results to combine.

This way, the job gets recursively split into smaller parts such as an inverted tree, until the smallest part can be carried out in just a single thread. When the leaf/subtree jobs return, the parent combines the result of all children, and returns the results.

The fork/join framework is implemented in Java 7 in terms of a special kind of thread pool; check out `java.util.concurrent.ForkJoinPool`. The specialty of this thread pool is that it accepts the jobs of `java.util.concurrent.ForkJoinTask` type, and whenever these jobs block, waiting for the child jobs to finish, the threads used by the waiting jobs are allocated to the child jobs. When the child finishes its work, the thread is allocated back to the blocked parent jobs in order to continue. This style of dynamic thread allocation is described as "work-stealing". The fork/join framework can be used from within Clojure. The `ForkJoinTask` interface has two implementations: `RecursiveAction` and `RecursiveTask` in the `java.util.concurrent` package. Concretely, `RecursiveTask` maybe more useful with Clojure, as `RecursiveAction` is designed to work with mutable data, and does not return any value from its operation.

Using the fork-join framework entails choosing the batch size to split a job into, which is a crucial factor in parallelizing a long job. Too large a batch size may not utilize all the CPU cores enough; on the other hand, a small batch size may lead to a longer overhead, coordinating across the parent/child batches. As we will see in the next section, Clojure integrates with the Fork/join framework to parallelize the reducers implementation.

Parallelism with reducers

Reducers are a new abstraction introduced in Clojure 1.5, and are likely to have a wider impact on the rest of the Clojure implementation in the future versions. They depict a different way of thinking about processing collections in Clojure—the key concept is to break down the notion that collections can be processed only sequentially, lazily, or producing a seq, and more. Moving away from such a behavior guarantee raises the potential for eager and parallel operations on one hand, whereas incurring constraints on the other. Reducers are compatible with the existing collections.

For an example, a keen observation of the regular map function reveals that its classic definition is tied to the mechanism (recursion), order (sequential), laziness (often), and representation (list/seq/other) aspects of producing the result. Most of this actually defines "how" the operation is performed, rather than "what" needs to be done. In the case of map, the "what" is all about applying a function to each element of its collection arguments. But since the collection types can be of various types (tree-structured, sequence, iterator, and more), the operating function cannot know how to navigate the collection. Reducers decouple the "what" and "how" parts of the operation.

Reducible, reducer function, reduction transformation

Collections are of various kinds, hence only a collection knows how to navigate itself. In the reducers model at a fundamental level, an internal "reduce" operation in each collection type has access to its properties and behavior, and access to what it returns. This makes all the collection types essentially "reducible". All the operations that work with collections can be modeled in terms of the internal "reduce" operation. The new modeled form of such operations is a "reducing function", which is typically a function of two arguments, the first argument being the accumulator, and the second being the new input.

How does it work when we need to layer several functions upon another, over the elements of a collection? For an example, let's say first we need to "filter", "map," and then "reduce". In such cases, a "transformation function" is used to model a reducer function (for example, for "filter") as another reducer function (for "map") in such a way that it adds the functionality during the transformation. This is called "reduction transformation".

Realizing reducible collections

While the reducer functions retain the purity of the abstraction, they are not useful all by themselves. The reducer operations in the namespace called as clojure.core.reducers similar to map, filter, and more, basically return a reducible collection that embed the reducer functions within themselves. A reducible collection is not realized, not even lazily realized—rather, it is just a recipe that is ready to be realized. In order to realize a reducible collection, we must use one of the reduce or fold operations.

The `reduce` operation that realizes a reducible collection is strictly sequential, albeit with the performance gains compared to `clojure.core/reduce`, due to reduced object allocations on the heap. The `fold` operation, which realizes a reducible collection, is potentially parallel, and uses a "reduce-combine" approach over the fork-join framework. Unlike the traditional "map-reduce" style, the use of fork/join the reduce-combine approach reduces at the bottom, and subsequently combines by the means of reduction again. This makes the `fold` implementation less wasteful and better performing.

Foldable collections and parallelism

Parallel reduction by `fold` puts certain constraints on the collections and operations. The tree-based collection types (persistent map, persistent vector, and persistent set) are amenable to parallelization. At the same time, the sequences may not be parallelized by `fold`. Secondly, `fold` requires that the individual reducer functions should be "associative", that is, the order of the input arguments applied to the reducer function should not matter. The reason being, `fold` can segment the elements of the collection to process in parallel, and the order in which they may be combined is not known in advance.

The `fold` function accepts few extra arguments, such as the "combine function," and the partition batch size (default being 512) for the parallel processing. Choosing the optimum partition size depends on the jobs, host capabilities, and the performance benchmarking. There are certain functions that are foldable (that is, parallelizable by `fold`), and there are others that are not, as shown here. They live in the `clojure.core.reducers` namespace:

- **Foldable**: `map`, `mapcat`, `filter`, `remove`, and `flatten`
- **Non-foldable**: `take-while`, `take`, and `drop`
- **Combine functions**: `cat`, `foldcat`, and `monoid`

A notable aspect of reducers is that it is foldable in parallel only when the collection is a tree type. This implies that the entire data set must be loaded in the heap memory when folding over them. This has the downside of memory consumption during the high load on a system. On the other hand, a lazy sequence is a perfectly reasonable solution for such scenarios. When processing large amount of data, it may make sense to use a combination of lazy sequences and reducers for performance.

Summary

Concurrency and parallelism are extremely important for performance in this multi-core age. Effective use of concurrency requires substantial understanding of the underlying principles and details. Fortunately, Clojure provides safe and elegant ways to deal with concurrency and state. Clojure's new feature called "reducers" provides a way to achieve granular parallelism. In the coming years, we are likely to see more and more processor cores, and an increasing demand to write code that takes advantage of these. Clojure places us in the right spot to meet such challenges.

In the next chapter, we will look at the performance measurement, analysis, and monitoring.

6
Measuring Performance

Depending on the expected and actual performance, and the lack or presence of a measuring system, performance analysis and tuning can be a fairly elaborate process. Now we will discuss the analysis of performance characteristics and ways to measure and monitor them. In this chapter we will cover the following topics:

- Measuring performance and understanding the results
- What performance tests to carry out for different purposes
- Monitoring performance and obtaining metrics
- Profiling Clojure code to identify performance bottlenecks

Performance measurement and statistics

Measuring performance is the stepping stone to performance analysis. As we noted earlier in this book, there are several performance parameters to be measured with respect to various scenarios. Clojure's built-in `time` macro is a tool to measure the amount of time elapsed while executing a body of code. Measuring performance factors is a much more involved process. The measured performance numbers may have linkages with each other that we need to analyze. It is a common practice to use statistical concepts to establish the linkage factors. We will discuss some basic statistical concepts in this section and use that to explain how the measured data gives us the bigger picture.

A tiny statistics terminology primer

When we have a series of quantitative data, such as latency in milliseconds for the same operation (measured over a number of executions), we can observe a number of things. First, and the most obvious, are the minimum and maximum values in the data. Let's take an example dataset to analyze further:

23	19	21	24	26	20	22	21	25	168	23	20	29	172	22	24	26

Median, first quartile, third quartile

We can see that the minimum latency here is 19 ms whereas the maximum latency is 172ms. We can also observe that the average latency here is about 40ms. Let's sort this data in ascending order:

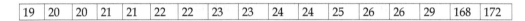

19	20	20	21	21	22	22	23	23	24	24	25	26	26	29	168	172

The center element of the previous dataset, that is the ninth element (value 23), is considered the **median** of the dataset. It is noteworthy that the median is a better representative of the center of the data than the **average** or **mean**. The center element of the left half, that is the fifth element (value 21), is considered the **first quartile**. Similarly, the value in the center of the right half, that is the 13th element (value 26), is considered the **third quartile** of the dataset. The difference between the third quartile and the first quartile is called **Inter Quartile Range (IQR)**, which is 5 in this case. This can be illustrated with a **boxplot**, as follows:

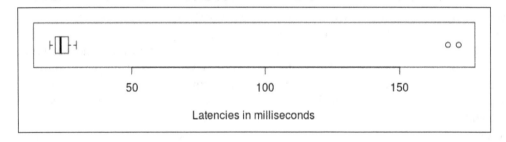

Latencies in milliseconds

A boxplot highlights the first quartile, median and the third quartile of a dataset. As you can see, two "outlier" latency numbers (168 and 172) are unusually higher than the others. Median makes no representation of outliers in a dataset, whereas the mean does.

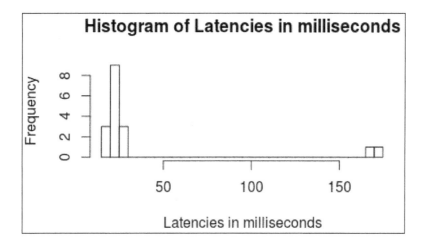

A histogram (the diagram shown previously) is another way to display a dataset where we batch the data elements in **periods** and expose the **frequency** of such periods. A period contains the elements in a certain range. All periods in a histogram are generally the same size; however, it is not uncommon to omit certain periods when there is no data.

Percentile

A **percentile** is expressed with a parameter, such as 99 percentile, or 95 percentile etc. A percentile is the value below which all the specified percentage of data elements exist. For example, 95 percentile means the value N among a dataset, such that 95 percent of elements in the dataset are below N in value. As a concrete example, 85 percentile from the dataset of latency numbers we discussed earlier in this section is 29, because out of 17 total elements, 14 (which is 85 percent of 17) other elements in the dataset have a value below 29. A quartile splits a dataset into chunks of 25 percent elements each. Therefore, the first quartile is actually 25 percentile, the median is 50 percentile, and the third quartile is 75 percentile.

Variance and standard deviation

The spread of the data, that is, how far away the data elements are from the center value, gives us further insight into the data. Consider the ith deviation as the difference between the ith dataset element value (in statistics terms, a "variable" value) and its mean; we can represent it as $x_i - \bar{x}$. We can express its "variance" and "standard deviation" as follows:

$$\text{Variance} = \sum_{i=1}^{a}(x_i - \bar{x})^2, \text{ standard deviation } (\sigma) = \sqrt{variance} = \sqrt{\frac{\sum_{i=1}^{a}(x_i - \bar{x})^2}{n-1}}$$

Standard deviation is shown as the Greek letter "sigma", or simply "s". Consider the following Clojure code to determine variance and standard deviation:

```
(def tdata [23 19 21 24 26 20 22 21 25 168 23 20 29 172 22 24 26])

(defn var-std-dev
  "Return variance and standard deviation in a vector"
  [data]
  (let [size (count data)
        mean (/ (reduce + data) size)
        sum (->> data
                 (map #(let [v (- % mean)] (* v v)))
                 (reduce +))
        variance (double (/ sum (dec size)))]
    [variance (Math/sqrt variance)]))

user=> (println (var-std-dev tdata))
[2390.345588235294 48.89116063497873]
```

You can use the Clojure-based platform Incanter (http://incanter.org/) for statistical computations. For example, you can find standard deviation using (incanter.stats/sd tdata) in Incanter.

The **empirical rule** states the relationship between the elements of a dataset and SD. It says that 68.3 percent of all elements in a dataset lie in the range of one (positive or negative) SD from the mean, 95.5 percent of all elements lie in two SDs from the mean, and 99.7 percent of all data elements lie in three SDs from the mean.

Looking at the latency dataset we started out with, one SD from the mean is 40 ± 49 (40 ± 98 range -9 to 89) containing 88 percent of all elements. Two SDs from the mean is 40 ± 49 range -58 to 138) containing the same 88 percent of all elements. However, three SDs from the mean is(40 ± 147 range -107 to 187) containing 100 percent of all elements. There is a mismatch between what the empirical rule states and the results we found, because the empirical rule applies generally to uniformly distributed datasets with a large number of elements.

Understanding Criterium output

In *Chapter 4, Host Performance*, we introduced the Clojure library *Criterium* to measure the latency of Clojure expressions. A sample benchmarking result is as follows:

```
user=> (require '[criterium.core :refer [bench]])
nil
user=> (bench (reduce + (range 1000)))
Evaluation count : 162600 in 60 samples of 2710 calls.
             Execution time mean : 376.756518 us
    Execution time std-deviation : 3.083305 us
   Execution time lower quantile : 373.021354 us ( 2.5%)
   Execution time upper quantile : 381.687904 us (97.5%)

Found 3 outliers in 60 samples (5.0000 %)
low-severe 2 (3.3333 %)
low-mild 1 (1.6667 %)
 Variance from outliers : 1.6389 % Variance is slightly inflated by
outliers
```

We can see that the result has some familiar terms we discussed earlier in this section. A high mean and low standard deviation indicate that there is not a lot of variation in the execution times. Likewise, the lower (first) and upper (third) quartiles indicate that they are not too far away from the mean. This result implies that the body of code is more or less stable in terms of response time. Criterium repeats the execution many times to collect the latency numbers.

However, why does Criterium attempt to do a statistical analysis of the execution time? What would be amiss if we simply calculate the mean? It turns out that the response times of all executions are not always stable and there is often disparity in how the response time shows up. Only upon running sufficient times under correctly simulated load we can get complete data and other indicators about the latency. A statistical analysis gives insight into whether there is something wrong with the benchmark.

Guided performance objectives

We only briefly discussed performance objectives in *Chapter 1*, *Performance by Design* because that discussion needs a reference to statistical concepts. Let's say we identified the functional scenarios and the corresponding response time. Should response time remain fixed? Can we constrain throughput in order to prefer a stipulated response time?

The performance objective should specify the worst-case response time, that is, maximum latency, the average response time and the maximum standard deviation. Similarly, the performance objective should also mention the worst-case throughput, maintenance window throughput, average throughput, and the maximum standard deviation.

Performance testing

Testing for performance requires us to know what we are going to test, how we want to test, and what environment to set up for the tests to execute. There are several pitfalls to be aware of, such as a lack of near-real hardware and resources of production use, similar OS and software environments, diversity of representative data for test cases, and so on. Lack of diversity in test inputs may lead to a monotonic branch prediction, hence introducing a "bias" in test results.

The test environment

Concerns about the test environment begin with the hardware representative of the production environment. Traditionally, the test environment hardware has been a scaled-down version of the production environment. The performance analysis done on non-representative hardware is almost certain to skew the results. Fortunately, in recent times, thanks to the commodity hardware and cloud systems, provisioning test environment hardware that is similar to the production environment is not too difficult.

The network and storage bandwidth, operating system, and software used for performance testing should of course be the same as in production. What is also important is to have a "load" representative of the test scenarios. The load comes in different combinations including the concurrency of requests, the throughput and standard deviation of requests, the current population level in the database or in the message queue, CPU and heap usage, and so on. It is important to simulate a representative load.

Testing often requires quite some work on the part of the piece of code that carries out the test. Be sure to keep its overhead to a minimum so that it does not impact the benchmark results. Wherever possible, use a system other than the test target to generate requests.

What to test

Any implementation of a non-trivial system typically involves many hardware and software components. Performance testing a certain feature or a service in the entire system needs to account for the way it interacts with the various sub-systems. For example, a web service call may touch multiple layers such as the web server (request/response marshaling and unmarshaling), URI-based routing, service handler, application-database connector, the database layer, logger component, and so on. Testing only the service handler would be a terrible mistake, because that is not exactly the performance what the web client will experience. The performance test should test at the perimeter of a system to keep the results realistic, preferably with a third-party observer.

The performance objectives state the criteria for testing. It would be useful to test what is not required by the objective, especially when the tests are run concurrently. Running meaningful performance tests may require a certain level of isolation.

Measuring latency

The latency obtained by executing a body of code may vary slightly on each run. This necessitates that we execute the code many times and collect samples. The latency numbers may be impacted by the JVM warm-up time, garbage collection and the JIT compiler kicking in. So, the test and sample collection should ensure that these conditions do not impact the results. Criterium follows such methods to produce the results. When we test a very small piece of code this way, it is called a **Micro-benchmark**.

As the latency of some operations may vary during runs, it is important to collect all samples and segregate them into periods and frequencies turning up into a histogram. The maximum latency is an important metric when measuring latency — it indicates the worst-case latency. Besides the maximum, the 99 percentile and 95 percentile latency numbers are also important to put things in perspective. It's important to actually collect the latency numbers instead of inferring them from standard deviation, as we noted earlier that the empirical rule works only for normal distributions without significant outliers.

The outliers are an important data point when measuring latency. A proportionately higher count of outliers indicates a possibility of degradation of service.

Comparative latency measurement

When evaluating libraries for use in projects, or when coming up with alternate solutions against some baseline, comparative latency benchmarks are useful to determine the performance trade-offs. We will inspect two comparative benchmarking tools based on Criterium, called Perforate and Citius. Both make it easy to run Criterium benchmarks grouped by context, and to easily view the benchmark results.

Perforate (`https://github.com/davidsantiago/perforate`) is a Leiningen plugin that lets one define goals; a goal (defined using `perforate.core/defgoal`) is a common task or context having one or more benchmarks. Each benchmark is defined using `perforate.core/defcase`. As of version 0.3.4, a sample benchmark code may look like the following code snippet:

```
(ns foo.bench
  (:require [perforate.core :as p]))

(p/defgoal str-concat "String concat")
(p/defcase str-concat :apply
  [] (apply str ["foo" "bar" "baz"]))
(p/defcase str-concat :reduce
  [] (reduce str ["foo" "bar" "baz"]))

(p/defgoal sum-numbers "Sum numbers")
(p/defcase sum-numbers :apply
  [] (apply + [1 2 3 4 5 6 7 8 9 0]))
(p/defcase sum-numbers :reduce
  [] (reduce + [1 2 3 4 5 6 7 8 9 0]))
```

You can declare the test environments in `project.clj` and provide the setup/cleanup code when defining the goal. Perforate provides ways to run the benchmarks from the command-line.

Citius (`https://github.com/kumarshantanu/citius`) is a library that provides integration hooks for clojure.test and other forms of invocation. It imposes more rigid constraints than Perforate, and renders additional comparative information about the benchmarks. It presumes a fixed number of targets (cases) per test suite where there may be several goals.

As of version 0.2.1, a sample benchmark code may look like the following code snippet:

```
(ns foo.bench
  (:require [citius.core :as c]))

(c/with-bench-context ["Apply" "Reduce"]
  {:chart-title "Apply vs Reduce"
   :chart-filename "bench-simple.png"}
  (c/compare-perf
    "concat strs"
    (apply str ["foo" "bar" "baz"])
    (reduce str ["foo" "bar" "baz"]))
  (c/compare-perf
    "sum numbers"
    (apply + [1 2 3 4 5 6 7 8 9 0])
    (reduce + [1 2 3 4 5 6 7 8 9 0])))
```

In the previous example, the code runs the benchmarks, reports the comparative summary, and draws a bar chart image of the mean latencies.

Latency measurement under concurrency

When we benchmark a piece of code with Criterium, it uses just a single thread to determine results. That gives us a fair output in terms of single-threaded result, but there are many benchmarking scenarios where single-threaded latency is far from what we need. Under concurrency, the latency often differs quite a bit from single-threaded latency. Especially when we deal with *stateful* objects (e.g. drawing a connection from a JDBC connection pool, updating shared in-memory state etc.), the latency is likely to vary in proportion with the contention. In such scenarios it is useful to find out the latency patterns of the code under various concurrency levels.

The Citius library we discussed in the previous sub-section supports tunable concurrency levels. Consider the following benchmark of implementations of shared counters:

```
(ns foo.bench
  (:require
    [clojure.test :refer [deftest]]
    [citius.core :as c])
  (:import [java.util.concurrent.atomic AtomicLong]))

(def a (atom 0))
(def ^AtomicLong b (AtomicLong. 0))
```

```
(deftest test-counter
  (c/with-bench-context ["Atom" "AtomicLong"] {}
    (c/compare-perf "counter"
      (swap! a unchecked-inc) (.incrementAndGet b))))

;; Under Unix-like systems run the following command in terminal:
;; CITIUS_CONCURRENCY=4,4 lein test
```

When I ran this benchmark on a 4th generation quad-core Intel Core i7 processor (Mac OSX 10.10), the mean latency at concurrency level 04 was 38 to 42 times the value of the mean latency at concurrency level 01. Since, in many cases, the JVM is used to run server-side applications, benchmarking under concurrency becomes all the more important.

Measuring throughput

Throughput is expressed per unit of time. Coarse-grained throughput, that is, the throughput number collected over a long period of time, may hide the fact when the throughput is actually delivered in bursts instead of a uniform distribution. Granularity of the throughput test is subject to the nature of the operation. A batch process may process bursts of data, whereas a web service may deliver uniformly distributed throughput.

Average throughput test

Though Citius (as of version 0.2.1) shows extrapolated throughput (per second, per thread) in benchmark results, that throughput number may not represent the actual throughput very well for a variety of reasons. Let's construct a simple throughput benchmark harness as follows, beginning with the helper functions:

```
(import '[java.util.concurrent ExecutorService Executors Future])
(defn concurrently
  ([n f]
    (concurrently n f #(mapv deref %)))
  ([n f g]
    (let [^ExecutorService
          thread-pool (Executors/newFixedThreadPool n)
          future-vals (transient [])]
      (dotimes [i n]
        (let [^Callable task (if (coll? f) (nth f i) f)
              ^Future each-future (.submit thread-pool task)]
          (conj! future-vals each-future)))
```

```
      (try
        (g (persistent! future-vals))
        (finally
          (.shutdown thread-pool))))))))

(defn call-count
  []
  (let [stats (atom 0)]
    (fn
      ([] (deref stats))
      ([k] (if (identical? :reset k)
             (reset! stats 0)
             (swap! stats unchecked-inc))))))

(defn wrap-call-stats
  [stats f]
  (fn [& args]
    (try
      (let [result (apply f args)]
        (stats :count)
        result))))

(defn wait-until-millis
  ([^long timeout-millis]
    (wait-until-millis timeout-millis 100))
  ([^long timeout-millis ^long progress-millis]
    (while (< (System/currentTimeMillis) timeout-millis)
      (let [millis (min progress-millis
                        (- timeout-millis (System/currentTimeMillis)))]
        (when (pos? millis)
          (try
            (Thread/sleep millis)
            (catch InterruptedException e
              (.interrupt ^Thread (Thread/currentThread)))))
        (print \.)
        (flush)))))
```

Now that we have the helper functions defined, let's see the benchmarking code:

```
(defn benchmark-throughput*
  [^long concurrency ^long warmup-millis ^long bench-millis f]
  (let [now        #(System/currentTimeMillis)
        exit?      (atom false)
```

```
              stats-coll (repeatedly concurrency call-count)
              g-coll     (->> (repeat f)
                              (map wrap-call-stats stats-coll)
                              (map-indexed (fn [i g]
                                               (fn []
                                                 (let [r (nth stats-coll i)]
                                                   (while (not (deref exit?))
                                                     (g))
                                                   (r)))))
                              vec)
              call-count (->> (fn [future-vals]
                                (print "\nWarming up")
                                (wait-until-millis (+ (now) warmup-millis))
                                (mapv #(% :reset) stats-coll) ; reset count
                                (print "\nBenchmarking")
                                (wait-until-millis (+ (now) bench-millis))
                                (println)
                                (swap! exit? not)
                                (mapv deref future-vals))
                              (concurrently concurrency g-coll)
                              (apply +))]
         {:concurrency concurrency
          :calls-count call-count
          :duration-millis bench-millis
          :calls-per-second (->> (/ bench-millis 1000)
                                 double
                                 (/ ^long call-count)
                                 long)}))

(defmacro benchmark-throughput
  "Benchmark a body of code for average throughput."
  [concurrency warmup-millis bench-millis & body]
  `(benchmark-throughput*
    ~concurrency ~warmup-millis ~bench-millis (fn [] ~@body)))
```

Let's now see how to test some code for throughput using the harness:

```
(def a (atom 0))
(println
  (benchmark-throughput
    4 20000 40000 (swap! a inc)))
```

This harness provides only a simple throughput test. To inspect the throughput pattern you may want to bucket the throughput across rolling fixed-duration windows (e.g. per second throughput.) However, that topic is beyond the scope of this text, though we will touch upon it in the *Performance monitoring* section later in this chapter.

The load, stress, and endurance tests

One of the characteristics of tests is each run only represents the slice of time it is executed through. Repeated runs establish their general behavior. But how many runs should be enough? There may be several anticipated load scenarios for an operation. So, there is a need to repeat the tests at various load scenarios. Simple test runs may not always exhibit the long-term behavior and response of the operation. Running the tests under varying high load for longer duration allows us to observe them for any odd behavior that may not show up in a short test cycle.

When we test an operation at a load far beyond its anticipated latency and throughput objectives, that is **stress testing**. The intent of a stress test is to ascertain a reasonable behavior exhibited by the operation beyond the maximum load it was developed for. Another way to observe the behavior of an operation is to see how it behaves when run for a very long duration, typically for several days or weeks. Such prolonged tests are called **endurance tests**. While a stress test checks the graceful behavior of the operation, an endurance test checks the consistent behavior of the operation over a long period.

There are several tools that may help with load and stress testing. Engulf (`http://engulf-project.org/`) is a distributed HTTP-based, load-generation tool written in Clojure. Apache JMeter and Grinder are Java-based load-generation tools. Grinder can be scripted using Clojure. Apache Bench is a load-testing tool for web systems. Tsung is an extensible, high-performance, load-testing tool written in Erlang.

Performance monitoring

During prolonged testing or after the application has gone to production, we need to monitor its performance to make sure the application continues to meet the performance objectives. There may be infrastructure or operational issues impacting the performance or availability of the application, or occasional spikes in latency or dips in throughput. Generally, monitoring alleviates such risk by generating a continuous feedback stream.

Roughly there are three kinds of components used to build a monitoring stack. A **collector** sends the numbers from each host that needs to be monitored. The collector gets host information and the performance numbers and sends them to an **aggregator**. An aggregator receives the data sent by the collector and persists them until asked by a **visualizer** on behalf of the user.

The project **metrics-clojure** (https://github.com/sjl/metrics-clojure) is a Clojure wrapper over the **Metrics** (https://github.com/dropwizard/metrics) Java framework, which acts as a collector. **Statsd** is a well-known aggregator that does not persist data by itself but passes it on to a variety of servers. One of the popular visualizer projects is **Graphite** that stores the data as well as produces graphs for requested periods. There are several other alternatives to these, notably **Riemann** (http://riemann.io/) that is written in Clojure and Ruby. Riemann is an event processing-based aggregator.

Monitoring through logs

One of the popular performance monitoring approaches that has emerged in recent times is via logs. The idea is simple—the application emits metrics data as logs, which are shipped from the individual machine to a central log aggregation service. Then, those metrics data are aggregated for each time window and further moved for archival and visualization.

As a high-level example of such a monitoring system, you may like to use **Logstash-forwarder** (https://github.com/elastic/logstash-forwarder) to grab the application logs from the local filesystem and ship to **Logstash** (https://www.elastic.co/products/logstash), where it forwards the metrics logs to **StatsD** (https://github.com/etsy/statsd) for metrics aggregation or to Riemann (http://riemann.io/) for events analysis and monitoring alerts. StatsD and/or Riemann can forward the metrics data to Graphite (http://graphite.wikidot.com/) for archival and graphing of the time-series metrics data. Often, people want to plug in a non-default time-series data store (such as **InfluxDB**: https://influxdb.com/) or a visualization layer (such as **Grafana**: http://grafana.org/) with Graphite.

A detailed discussion on this topic is out of the scope of this text, but I think exploring this area would serve you well.

Ring (web) monitoring

If you develop web software using Ring (`https://github.com/ring-clojure/ring`) then you may find the Ring extension of the metrics-clojure library useful: `http://metrics-clojure.readthedocs.org/en/latest/ring.html` — this tracks a number of useful metrics that can be queried in JSON format and integrated with visualization via the web browser.

To emit a continuous stream of metrics data from the web layer, **Server-Sent Events** (**SSE**) may be a good idea due to its low overhead. Both **http-kit** (`http://www.http-kit.org/`) and **Aleph** (`http://aleph.io/`), which work with Ring, support SSE today.

Introspection

Both Oracle JDK and OpenJDK provide two GUI tools called **JConsole** (executable name `jconsole`) and **JVisualVM** (executable name `jvisualvm`) that we can use to introspect into running JVMs for instrumentation data. There are also some command-line tools (`http://docs.oracle.com/javase/8/docs/technotes/tools/`) in the JDK to peek into the inner details of the running JVMs.

A common way to introspect a running Clojure application is to have an **nREPL** (`https://github.com/clojure/tools.nrepl`) service running so that we can connect to it later using an nREPL client. Interactive introspection over nREPL using the Emacs editor (embedded nREPL client) is popular among some, whereas others prefer to script an nREPL client to carry out tasks.

JVM instrumentation via JMX

The JVM has a built-in mechanism to introspect managed resources via the extensible **Java Management Extensions** (**JMX**) API. It provides a way for application maintainers to expose manageable resources as "MBeans". Clojure has an easy-to-use `contrib` library called `java.jmx` (`https://github.com/clojure/java.jmx`) to access JMX. There is a decent amount of open source tooling for visualization of JVM instrumentation data via JMX, such as `jmxtrans` and `jmxetric`, which integrate with Ganglia and Graphite.

Getting quick memory stats of the JVM is pretty easy using Clojure:

```
(let [^Runtime r (Runtime/getRuntime)]
  (println "Maximum memory" (.maxMemory r))
  (println "Total memory" (.totalMemory r))
  (println "Free memory" (.freeMemory r)))
Output:
Maximum memory 704643072
Total memory 291373056
Free memory 160529752
```

Profiling

We briefly discussed profiler types in *Chapter 1, Performance by Design*. The JVisualVM tool we discussed with respect to introspection in the previous section is also a CPU and memory profiler that comes bundled with the JDK. Let's see them in action— consider the following two Clojure functions that stress the CPU and memory respectively:

```
(defn cpu-work []
  (reduce + (range 100000000)))

(defn mem-work []
  (->> (range 1000000)
       (map str)
       vec
       (map keyword)
       count))
```

Using JVisualVM is pretty easy—open the Clojure JVM process from the left pane. It has sampler and regular profiler styles of profiling. Start profiling for CPU or memory use when the code is running and wait for it to collect enough data to plot on the screen.

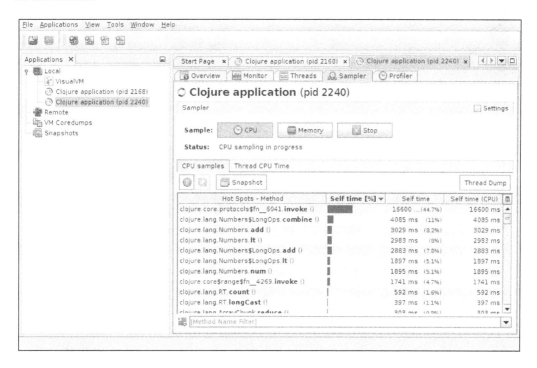

The following shows memory profiling in action:

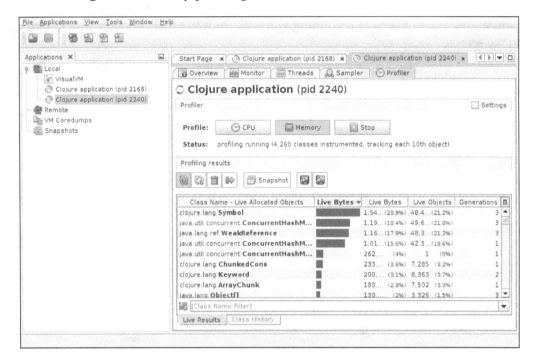

Note that JVisualVM is a very simple, entry-level profiler. There are several commercial JVM profilers on the market for sophisticated needs.

OS and CPU/cache-level profiling

Profiling only the JVM may not always tell the whole story. Getting down to OS and hardware-level profiling often provides better insight into what is going on with the application. On Unix-like operating systems, command-line tools such as `top`, `htop`, `perf`, `iota`, `netstat`, `vista`, `upstate`, `pidstat` etc can help. Profiling the CPU for cache misses and other information is a useful source to catch performance issues. Among open source tools for Linux, **Likwid** (`http://code.google.com/p/likwid/` and `https://github.com/rrze-likwid/likwid`) is small yet effective for Intel and AMD processors; **i7z** (`https://code.google.com/p/i7z/` and `https://github.com/ajaiantilal/i7z`) is specifically for Intel processors. There are also dedicated commercial tools such as **Intel VTune Analyzer** for more elaborate needs.

I/O profiling

Profiling I/O may require special tools too. Besides `iota` and `blktrace`, `ioping` (`https://code.google.com/p/ioping/` and `https://github.com/koct9i/ioping`) is useful to measure real-time I/O latency on Linux/Unix systems. The **vnStat** tool is useful to monitor and log network traffic on Linux. The IOPS of a storage device may not tell the whole truth unless it is accompanied by latency information for different operations, and how many reads and writes can simultaneously happen.

In an I/O bound workload one has to look for the read and write IOPS over time and set a threshold to achieve optimum performance. The application should throttle the I/O access so that the threshold is not crossed.

Summary

Delivering high-performance applications not only requires care for performance but also systematic effort to measure, test, monitor, and optimize the performance of various components and subsystems. These activities often require the right skill and experience. Sometimes, performance considerations may even bring system design and architecture back to the drawing board. Early structured steps taken to achieve performance go a long way to ensuring that the performance objectives are being continuously met.

In the next chapter, we will look into performance optimization tools and techniques.

7
Performance Optimization

Performance optimization is additive by nature, as in it works by adding performance tuning to the knowledge of how the underlying system works, and to the result of performance measurement. This chapter builds on the previous ones that covered "how the underlying system works" and "performance measurement". Though you will notice some recipe-like sections in this chapter, you already know the pre-requisite in order to exploit those well. Performance tuning is an iterative process of measuring performance, determining bottlenecks, applying knowledge in order to experiment with tuning the code, and repeating it all until performance improves. In this chapter, we will cover:

- Setting up projects for better performance
- Identifying performance bottlenecks in the code
- Profiling code with VisualVM
- Performance tuning of Clojure code
- JVM performance tuning

Project setup

While finding bottlenecks is essential to fixing performance problems in the code, there are several things one can do right from the start to ensure better performance.

Software versions

Usually, new software versions include bug fixes, new features, and performance improvements. Unless advised to the contrary, it is better to use newer versions. For development with Clojure, consider the following software versions:

- **JVM version**: As of this writing, Java 8 (Oracle JDK, OpenJDK, Zulu) has been released as the latest stable production-ready version. It is not only stable, it also has better performance in several areas (especially concurrency) than the earlier versions. If you have a choice, choose Java 8 over the older versions of Java.

- **Clojure version**: As of this writing, Clojure 1.7.0 is the latest stable version that has several performance improvements over the older versions. There are also new features (transducers, volatile) that can make your code perform better. Choose Clojure 1.7 over the older versions unless you have no choice.

Leiningen project.clj configuration

As of version 2.5.1, the default Leiningen template (`lein new foo`, `lein new app foo`) needs few tweaks to make the project amenable to performance. Ensure your Leiningen `project.clj` file has the following entries, as appropriate.

Enable reflection warning

One of the most common pitfalls in Clojure programming is to inadvertently let the code resort to reflection. Recall that we discussed this in *Chapter 3, Leaning on Java*. *Enabling,* reflection warning is quite easy, let's fix it by adding the following entry to `project.clj`:

```
:global-vars {*unchecked-math* :warn-on-boxed ; in Clojure 1.7+
              *warn-on-reflection* true}
```

In the previous configuration, the first setting `*unchecked-math*` `:warn-on-boxed` works only in Clojure 1.7—it emits numeric boxing warnings. The second setting `*warn-on-reflection*` `true` works on earlier Clojure versions as well as Clojure 1.7, and emits reflection warning messages in the code.

However, including these settings in `project.clj` may not be enough. Reflection warnings are emitted only when a namespace is loaded. You need to ensure that all namespaces are loaded in order to search for reflection warnings throughout the project. This can be done by writing tests that refer to all namespaces, or via scripts that do so.

Enable optimized JVM options when benchmarking

In *Chapter 4*, *Host Performance* we discussed that Leiningen enables tiered compilation by default, which provides low startup time at the cost of poor JIT compiler optimization. The default setting is quite misleading for performance benchmarking, so you should enable JVM options that are representative of what you would use in production:

```
:profiles {:perf {:test-paths ^:replace ["perf-test"]
                  :jvm-opts ^:replace ["-server"
                                       "-Xms2048m" "-Xmx2048m"]}}
```

For example, the previous setting defines a Leiningen profile that overrides the default JVM options to configure a `server` Java runtime with 2 GB of fixed-size heap space. It also sets test paths to a directory `perf-test`. Now you can run performance tests as follows:

```
lein with-profile perf test
```

If your project has performance test suites that require different JVM options, you should define multiple profiles for running tests, as appropriate.

Distinguish between initialization and runtime

Most non-trivial projects need a lot of context to be set up before they can function. Examples of such contexts could be app configuration, in-memory state, I/O resources, thread pools, caches, and so on. While many projects start with ad hoc configuration and initialization, eventually projects need to isolate the initialization phase from runtime. The purpose of this distinction is not only to sanitize the organization of code, but also to pre-compute as much as possible once before the runtime can take over to repeatedly respond to demands. This distinction also allows the initialization phase to easily (and conditionally, based on configuration) instrument the initialized code for performance logging and monitoring.

Non-trivial programs are usually divided into layers, such as business logic, caching, messaging, database access, and so on. Each layer has a dependency relationship with one or more of the other layers. It is feasible to carry out the isolation of the initialization phase by writing code using first principles, and many projects actually do that. However, there are a few libraries that simplify this process by letting you declare the dependency relationship between layers. **Component** (`https://github.com/stuartsierra/component`) and **Prismatic Graph** (`https://github.com/Prismatic/plumbing`) are notable examples of such libraries.

The Component library is well documented. It may not be easily apparent how to use Prismatic Graph for dependency resolution; following is a contrived example for illustration:

```
(require '[plumbing.core :refer [fnk]])
(require '[plumbing.graph :as g])

(def layers
  {:db      (fnk [config]     (let [pool (db-pool config)]
                                  (reify IDatabase ...)))
   :cache   (fnk [config db] (let [cache-obj (mk-cache config)]
                                  (reify ICache    ...)))
   :service (fnk [config db cache] (reify IService  ...))
   :web     (fnk [config service]  (reify IWeb      ...))})

(defn resolve-layers
  "Return a map of reified layers"
  [app-config]
  (let [compiled (g/compile layers)]
    (compiled {:config app-config})))
```

This example merely shows the construction of a layer dependency graph, but often you may need different construction scope and order for testing. In that case you may define different graphs and resolve them, as and when appropriate. If you need teardown logic for testing, you can add extra fnk entries for each teardown step and use those for teardown.

Identifying performance bottlenecks

We discussed in previous chapters that random performance tuning of code rarely works, because we may not be tuning in the right place. It is crucial to find the performance bottlenecks before we can tune those areas in the code. Upon finding the bottleneck, we can experiment with alternate solutions around it. In this section we will look into finding the bottlenecks.

Latency bottlenecks in Clojure code

Latency is the starting, and the most obvious, metric to drill-down in order to find bottlenecks. For Clojure code, we observed in *Chapter 6, Measuring Performance* that code profiling tools can help us find the areas of bottleneck. Profilers are, of course, very useful. Once you discover hotspots via profilers, you may find ways to tune those for latency to a certain extent.

Most profilers work on aggregates, a batch of runs, ranking the hotspots in code by resources consumed. However, often the opportunity to tune latency lies in the long tail that may not be highlighted by the profilers. In such circumstances, we may employ a direct drill-down technique. Let's see how to carry out such drill-down using **Espejito** (`https://github.com/kumarshantanu/espejito`), a Clojure library for measuring latency (as of version 0.1.0) across measurement points in single-threaded execution paths. There are two parts of using **Espejito**, both requiring change to your code—one to wrap the code being measured, and the other to report the collected measurement data. The following code illustrates a contrived E-commerce use case of adding an item to a cart:

```clojure
(require '[espejito.core :as e])

;; in the top level handler (entry point to the use case)
(e/report e/print-table
  ...)

;; in web.clj
(e/measure "web/add-cart-item"
  (biz/add-item-to-cart (resolve-cart request) item-code qty)
  ...)

;; in service.clj (biz)
(defn add-item-to-cart
  [cart item qty]
  (e/measure "biz/add-cart-item"
    (db/save-cart-item (:id cart) (:id item) qty)
    ...))

;; in db.clj (db)
(defn save-cart-item
  [cart-id item-id qty]
  (e/measure "db/save-cart-item"
    ...))
```

Reporting a call is required to be made only once at the outermost (top-level) layer of the code. Measurement calls can be made at any number of places in the call path. Be careful not to put measurement calls inside tight loops, which may shoot memory consumption up. When this execution path is triggered, the functionality works as usual, while the latencies are measured and recorded alongside transparently in memory. The `e/report` call prints a table of recorded metrics. An example output (edited to fit) would be:

```
|                     :name|:cumulat|:cumul%|:indiv |:indiv%|:thrown?|
|--------------------+--------+-------+-------+-------+--------|
|     web/add-cart-item |11.175ms|100.00%|2.476ms|22.16% |        |
| biz/add-item-to-cart | 8.699ms| 77.84%|1.705ms|15.26% |        |
|     db/save-cart-item | 6.994ms| 62.59%|6.994ms|62.59% |        |
```

Here we can observe that the database call is the most expensive (individual latency), followed by the web layer. Our tuning preference may be guided by the order of expensiveness of the measurement points.

Measure only when it is hot

One important aspect we did not cover in the drill-down measurement is whether the environment is ready for measurement. The `e/report` call is invoked unconditionally every time, which would not only have its own overhead (table printing), but the JVM may not be warmed up and the JIT compiler may not have kicked in to correctly report the latencies. To ensure that we report only meaningful latencies, let's trigger the `e/report` call on an example condition:

```
(defmacro report-when
  [test & body]
  `(if ~test
    (e/report e/print-table
      ~@body)
    ~@body))
```

Now, let's assume it is a **Ring**-based (`https://github.com/ring-clojure/ring`) web app and you want to trigger the reporting only when the web request contains a parameter `report` with a value `true`. In that case, your call might look like the following:

```
(report-when (= "true" (get-in request [:params "report"]))
  ...)
```

Condition-based invocation expects the JVM to be up across several calls, so it may not work with command-line apps.

This technique can also be used in performance tests, where non-reporting calls may be made during a certain warm-up period, followed by a reporting call that provides its own reporter function instead of `e/print-table`. You may even write a sampling reporter function that aggregates the samples over a duration and finally reports the latency metrics. Not only for performance testing, you can use this for latency monitoring where the reporter function logs the metrics instead of printing a table, or sends the latency breakup to a metrics aggregation system.

Garbage collection bottlenecks

Since Clojure runs on the JVM, one has to be aware of the GC behavior in the application. You can print out the GC details at runtime by specifying the respective JVM options in `project.clj` or on the Java command-line:

```
:jvm-options ^:replace [..other options..
                "-verbose:gc" "-XX:+PrintGCDetails"
                "-XX:+PrintGC" "-XX:+PrintGCTimeStamps"
                ..other options..]
```

This causes a detailed summary of GC events to be printed as the application runs. To capture the output in a file, you can specify the following parameter:

```
:jvm-options ^:replace [..other options..
                "-verbose:gc" "-XX:+PrintGCDetails"
                "-XX:+PrintGC" "-XX:+PrintGCTimeStamps"
                "-Xloggc:./memory.log"
                ..other options..]
```

It is also useful to see the time between and during full GC events:

```
:jvm-options ^:replace [..other options..
                  "-verbose:gc" "-XX:+PrintGCDetails"
                  "-XX:+PrintGC" "-XX:+PrintGCTimeStamps"
                  "-XX:+PrintGCApplicationStoppedTime"
                  "-XX:+PrintGCApplicationConcurrentTime"
                  ..other options..]
```

The other useful options to troubleshoot GC are as follows:

- `-XX:+HeapDumpOnOutOfMemoryError`
- `-XX:+PrintTenuringDistribution`
- `-XX:+PrintHeapAtGC`

The output of the previous options may help you identify GC bottlenecks that you can try to fix by choosing the right garbage collector, other generational heap options, and code changes. For easy viewing of GC logs, you may like to use GUI tools such as **GCViewer** (`https://github.com/chewiebug/GCViewer`) for this purpose.

Threads waiting at GC safepoint

When there is a long tight loop (without any I/O operation) in the code, the thread executing it cannot be brought to safepoint if GC happens when the loop ends or goes out of memory (for example, fails to allocate). This may have a disastrous effect of stalling other critical threads during GC. You can identify this category of bottleneck by enabling safepoint logs using the following JVM option:

```
:jvm-options ^:replace [..other options..
                  "-verbose:gc" "-XX:+PrintGCDetails"
                  "-XX:+PrintGC" "-XX:+PrintGCTimeStamps"
                  "-XX:+PrintSafepointStatistics"
                  ..other options..]
```

The safepoint logs emitted by the previous option may help you identify the impact of a tight-loop thread on other threads during GC.

Using jstat to probe GC details

The Oracle JDK (also OpenJDK, Azul's Zulu) comes with a utility called `jstat` that can be handy to inspect GC details. You can find details on this utility at `https://docs.oracle.com/javase/8/docs/technotes/tools/unix/jstat.html` — the following examples show how to use it:

```
jstat -gc -t <process-id> 10000
jstat -gccause -t <process-id> 10000
```

The first command mentioned previously monitors object allocations and freeing in various heap generations, together with other GC statistics, one in every 10 seconds. The second command also prints the reason for GC, along with other details.

Inspecting generated bytecode for Clojure source

We discussed in *Chapter 3, Leaning on Java* how to see the generated equivalent Java code for any Clojure code. Sometimes, there may not be a direct correlation between the generated bytecode and Java, which is when inspecting the generated bytecode is very useful. Of course, it requires the reader to know at least a bit about the JVM instruction set (`http://docs.oracle.com/javase/specs/jvms/se8/html/jvms-6.html`). This tool can allow you to very effectively analyze the cost of the generated bytecode instructions.

The project **no.disassemble** (`https://github.com/gtrak/no.disassemble`) is a very useful tool to discover the generated bytecode. Include it in your `project.clj` file as a Leiningen plugin:

```
:plugins [[lein-nodisassemble "0.1.3"]]
```

Then, at the REPL, you can inspect the generated bytecodes one by one:

```
(require '[no.disassemble :as n])
(println (n/disassemble (map inc (range 10))))
```

The previous snippet prints out the bytecode of the Clojure expression entered there.

Throughput bottlenecks

The throughput bottlenecks usually arise from shared resources, which could be CPU, cache, memory, mutexes and locks, GC, disk, and other I/O devices. Each of these resources has a different way to find utilization, saturation, and load level. This also heavily depends on the operating system in use, as it manages the resources. Delving into the OS-specific ways of determining those factors is beyond the scope of this text. However, we will look at profiling some of these for bottlenecks in the next section.

The net effect of throughput shows up as an inverse relationship with latency. This is natural as per Little's law — as we will see in the next chapter. We covered throughput testing and latency testing under concurrency in *Chapter 6, Measuring Performance*. This should be roughly a good indicator of the throughput trend.

Profiling code with VisualVM

The Oracle JDK (also OpenJDK) comes with a powerful profiler called **VisualVM**; the distribution that comes with the JDK is known as Java VisualVM and can be invoked using the binary executable:

```
jvisualvm
```

This launches the GUI profiler app where you can connect to running instances of the JVM. The profiler has powerful features (`https://visualvm.java.net/features.html`) that can be useful for finding various bottlenecks in code. Besides analyzing heap dump and thread dump, VisualVM can interactively graph CPU and heap consumption, and thread status in near real time. It also has sampling and tracing profilers for both CPU and memory.

The Monitor tab

The **Monitor** tab has a graphical overview of the runtime, including CPU, heap, threads and loaded classes:

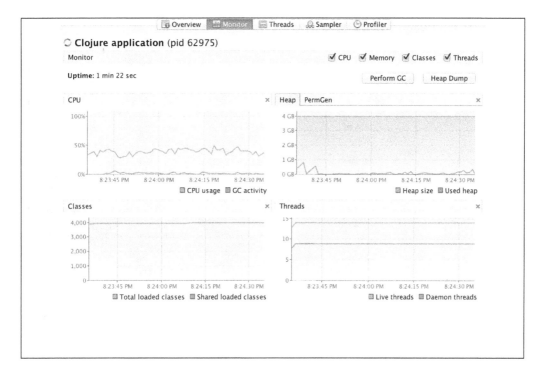

This tab is useful for "at a glance" information, leaving further drill-down for other tabs.

The Threads tab

In the following screenshot, the **Threads** tab shows the status of all threads:

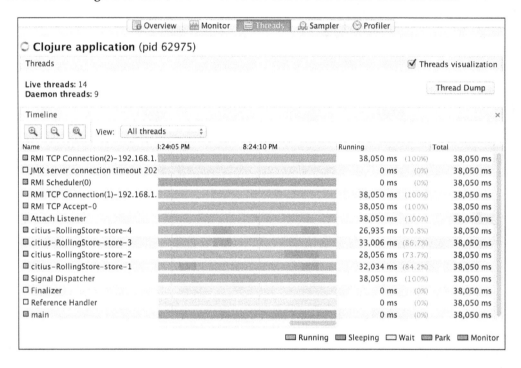

It is very useful to find out if any threads are undergoing contention, entering deadlock, are underutilized, or they are taking up more CPU. Especially in concurrent apps with in-memory state, and in apps that use limited I/O resources (such as connection pools, or network calls to other hosts) shared by threads, this feature provides a great insight if you set the thread names:

Notice the threads named **citius-RollingStore-store-1** through **citius-RollingStore-store - 4**. In an ideal no-contention scenario, those threads would have a green **Running** status. See the legend at the bottom right of the image, which explains thread state:

- **Running**: A thread is running, which is the ideal condition.

- **Sleeping**: A thread has yielded control temporarily.

- **Wait**: A thread is waiting for notification in a critical section. `Object.wait()` was called, and is now waiting for `Object.notify()` or `Object.notifyAll()` to wake it up.

- **Park**: A thread is parked on a permit (binary semaphore) waiting for some condition. Usually seen with concurrent blocking calls in the `java.util.concurrent` API.

- **Monitor**: A thread has reached object monitor waiting for some lock, perhaps waiting to enter or exit a critical section.

You can install the *Threads Inspector* plugin for details on threads of interest. To inspect thread dumps from the command line you can use the `jstack` or `kill -3` commands.

The Sampler tab

The **Sampler** tab is the lightweight sampling profiler tab that can sample both CPU and memory consumption. You can easily find hotspots in code that may benefit from tuning. However, sampler profiling is limited by sampling period and frequency, inability to detect inlined code, and so on. It is a good general indicator of the bottlenecks and looks similar to the screenshots we saw in *Chapter 6, Measuring Performance*. You can profile either CPU or memory at a time.

The **CPU** tab displays both the overall CPU time distribution and per-thread CPU consumption. You can take a thread dump while sampling is in progress and analyze the dump. There are several VisualVM plugins available for more analysis.

The **Memory** tab displays heap histogram metrics with distribution and instance count of objects. It also shows a PermGen histogram and per thread allocation data. It is a very good idea and highly recommended to set thread names in your project so that it is easy to locate those names in such tools. In this tab, you can force a GC, take a heap dump for analysis, and view memory metrics data in several ways.

Setting the thread name

Setting a thread name in Clojure is quite straightforward using Java interop:

```
(.setName ^Thread (Thread/currentThread) "service-thread-12")
```

However, since threads often transcend several contexts, in most cases you should do so in a limited scope as follows:

```
(defmacro with-thread-name
  "Set current thread name; execute body of code in that context."
  [new-name & body]
```

```
`(let [^Thread thread# (Thread/currentThread)
        ^String t-name# thread#]
    (.setName thread# ~new-name)
    (try
      ~@body
      (finally
        (.setName thread# t-name#)))
```

Now you can use this macro to execute any body of code with a specified thread name:

```
(with-thread-name (str "process-order-" order-id)
  ;; business code
  )
```

This style of setting a thread name makes sure that the original name is restored before leaving the thread-local scope. If your code has various sections and you are setting a different thread name for each section, you can detect which code sections are causing contention by looking at the name when any contention appears on profiling and monitoring tools.

The Profiler tab

The **Profiler** tab lets you instrument the running code in the JVM, and profile both CPU and memory consumption. This option adds a larger overhead than the **Sampler** tab, and poses a different trade off in terms of JIT compilation, inlining, and accuracy. This tab does not have as much diversity in visualization as the **Sampler** tab. The main difference this tab has with the **Sampler** tab is it changes the bytecode of the running code for accurate measurement. When you choose CPU profiling, it starts instrumenting the code for CPU profiling. If you switch from CPU to memory profiling, it re-instruments the running code for memory profiling, and re-instruments every time you want a different profiling. One downside of such instrumentation is that it may massively slow down everything if your code is deployed in application containers, such as Tomcat.

While you can get most of the common CPU bottleneck information from **Sampler**, you may need the **Profiler** to investigate hotspots already discovered by **Sampler** and other profiling techniques. You can selectively profile and drill-down only the known bottlenecks using the instrumenting profiler, thereby restricting its ill-effects to only small parts of the code.

The Visual GC tab

The **Visual GC** is a VisualVM plugin that visually depicts the GC status in near real time.

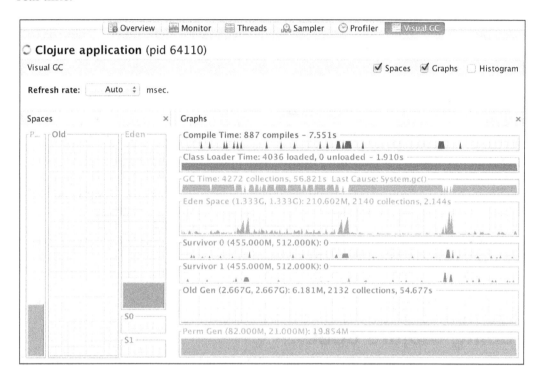

If your application uses a lot of memory and potentially has GC bottlenecks, this plugin may be very useful for various troubleshooting purposes.

The Alternate profilers

Besides VisualVM, there are several third-party profilers and performance-monitoring tools for the Java platform. Among open source tools, Prometheus (http://prometheus.io/) and Moskito (http://www.moskito.org/) are relatively popular. A non-exhaustive list of Open Source performance tools is here: http://java-source.net/open-source/profilers

There are several commercial proprietary profilers that you may want to know about. The YourKit (`https://www.yourkit.com/`) Java profiler is probably the most notable profiler that many people have found much success with for profiling Clojure code. There are also other profiling tools for the JVM, such as JProfiler (`https://www.ej-technologies.com/products/jprofiler/overview.html`), which is a desktop-based profiler and web-based hosted solutions such as New Relic (`http://newrelic.com/`) and AppDynamics (`https://www.appdynamics.com/`).

Performance tuning

Once we get insight into the code via testing and profiling results, we need to analyze the bottlenecks worth considering for optimization. A better approach is to find the most under-performing portion and optimize it, thereby eliminating the weakest link. We discussed performance aspects of hardware and JVM/Clojure in previous chapters. Optimization and tuning requires rethinking the design and code in light of those aspects, and then refactoring for performance objectives.

Once we establish the performance bottlenecks, we have to pinpoint the root cause and experiment with improvisations, one step at a time, to see what works. Tuning for performance is an iterative process that is backed by measurement, monitoring and experimentation.

Tuning Clojure code

Identifying the nature of the performance bottleneck helps a lot in order to experiment with the right aspects of the code. The key is to determine the origin of cost and whether the cost is reasonable.

CPU/cache bound

As we noted in the beginning of this chapter, setting up a project with the right JVM options and project settings informs us of reflection and boxing, the common sources of CPU-bound performance issues after poor design and algorithm choice. As a general rule, we have to see whether we are doing unnecessary or suboptimal operations, especially inside loops. For example, transducers are amenable to better performance than lazy sequences in CPU-bound operations.

While public functions are recommended to work with immutable data structures, the implementation details can afford to use transients and arrays when performance is necessary. Records are a great alternative to maps, where appropriate, due to type hints and tight field layout in the former. Operations on primitive data types is faster (hence recommended) than their boxed equivalents.

In tight loops, besides transients and arrays you may prefer loop-recur with unchecked math for performance. You may also like to avoid using multi-methods and dynamic vars in tight loops, rather than pass arguments around. Using Java and macros may be the last resort, but still an option if there is such a need for performance.

Memory bound

Allocating less memory in code is always going to reduce memory-related performance issues. Optimization of memory-bound code is not only about reducing memory consumption, but it is also about memory layout and utilizing the CPU and cache well. We have to see whether we are using the data types that fit well in CPU registers and cache lines. For cache and memory-bound code, we have to know whether there are cache misses and the reason—often the data might be too large to fit in a cache line. For memory-bound code we have to care about data locality, whether the code is hitting the interconnect too often, and whether memory representation of data can be slimmed down.

Multi-threaded

Shared resources with side effects are the main source of contention and performance bottlenecks in multi-threaded code. As we saw in the *Profiling VisualVM code* section in this chapter, profiling the threads better informs us about the bottlenecks. The best way to improve performance of multi-threaded code is to reduce contention. The easy way to reduce contention is to increase the resources and reduce concurrency, though only optimal levels of resources and concurrency would be good for performance. While designing for concurrency, append only, single writer, and shared nothing approaches work well.

Another way to reduce contention may be to exploit thread-local queueing of data until resources are available. This technique is similar to what Clojure agents use, though it is an involved technique. *Chapter 5, Concurrency* covers agents in some detail. I would encourage you to study the agents source code for better understanding. When using CPU-bound resources (for example `java.util.concurrent.atomic.AtomicLong`) you may use the contention-striping technique used by some Java 8 classes (such as `java.util.concurrent.atomic.LongAdder`, which also balances between memory consumption and contention striping across processors.) This technique is also quite involved and generic contention-striping solutions may have to trade off read consistency to allow fast updates.

I/O bound

I/O-bound tasks could be limited by bandwidth or IOPS/latency. Any I/O bottleneck usually manifests in chatty I/O calls or unconstrained data serialization. Restricting I/O to only minimum required data is a common opportunity to minimize serialization and reduce latency. I/O operations can often be batched for higher throughput, for example *SpyMemcached* library employs an asynchronous batched operation for high throughput.

I/O-bound bottlenecks are often coupled with multi-threaded scenarios. When the I/O calls are synchronous (for example, the JDBC API), one naturally has to depend upon multiple threads working on a bounded resource pool. Asynchronous I/O can relieve our threads from blocking, letting the threads do other useful work until the I/O response arrives. In synchronous I/O, we pay the cost of having threads (each allocated with memory) block on I/O calls while the kernel schedules them.

JVM tuning

Often Clojure applications might inherit bloat from Clojure/Java libraries or frameworks, which cause poor performance. Hunting down unnecessary abstractions and unnecessary layers of code may bring decent performance gains. Reasoning about the performance of dependency libraries/frameworks before inclusion in a project is a good approach.

The JIT compiler, garbage collector and safepoint (in Oracle HotSpot JVM) have a significant impact on the performance of applications. We discussed the JIT compiler and garbage collector in *Chapter 4, Host Performance*. When the HotSpot JVM reaches a point when it cannot carry out concurrent, incremental GC anymore, it needs to suspend the JVM safely in order to carry out a full GC. It is also called the stop-the-world GC pause that may run up to several minutes while the JVM appears frozen.

The Oracle and OpenJDK JVMs accept many command-line options when invoked, to tune and monitor the way components in the JVM behave. Tuning GC is common among people who want to extract optimum performance from the JVM.

You may like to experiment with the following JVM options (Oracle JVM or OpenJDK) for performance:

JVM option	Description
`-XX:+AggressiveOpts`	Aggressive options that enable compressed heap pointers
`-server`	Server class JIT thresholds (use -client for GUI apps)
`-XX:+UseParNewGC`	Use Parallel GC
`-Xms3g`	Specify min heap size (keep it less on desktop apps)
`-Xmx3g`	Specify max heap size (keep min/max same on servers)
`-XX:+UseLargePages`	Reduce Translation-Lookaside Buffer misses (if OS supports), see `http://www.oracle.com/technetwork/java/javase/tech/largememory-jsp-137182.html` for details

On the Java 6 HotSpot JVM, the **Concurrent Mark and Sweep** (**CMS**) garbage collector is well regarded for its GC performance. On the Java 7 and Java 8 HotSpot JVM, the default GC is a parallel collector (for better throughput), whereas at the time of writing this, there is a proposal to use the G1 collector (for lower pauses) by default in the upcoming Java 9. Note that the JVM GC can be tuned for different objectives, hence the same exact configuration for one application may not work well for another. Refer to the documents Oracle published for tuning the JVM at the following links:

- `http://www.oracle.com/technetwork/java/tuning-139912.html`
- `https://docs.oracle.com/javase/8/docs/technotes/guides/vm/gctuning/`

Back pressure

It is not uncommon to see applications behaving poorly under load. Typically, the application server simply appears unresponsive, which is often a combined result of high resource utilization, GC pressure, more threads that lead to busier thread scheduling, and cache misses. If the capacity of a system is known, the solution is to apply **back pressure** by denying services after the capacity is reached. Note that back pressure cannot be applied optimally until the system is load-tested for optimum capacity. The capacity threshold that triggers back pressure may or may not be directly associated with individual services, but rather can be defined as load criteria.

Summary

It is worth reiterating that performance optimization begins with learning about how the underlying system works, and measuring the performance of systems we build under representative hardware and load. The chief component of performance optimization is identifying the bottlenecks using various kinds of measurements and profiling. Thereafter, we can apply experiments to tune the performance of code and measure/profile once again to verify. The tuning mechanism varies depending on the type of bottleneck.

In the next chapter, we will see how to address performance concerns when building applications. Our focus will be on the several common patterns that impact performance.

8
Application Performance

The earliest computing devices were built to perform automatic computations and, as computers grew in power, they became increasingly popular because of how much and how fast they could compute. Even today, this essence lives on in our anticipation that computers can execute our business calculations faster than before by means of the applications we run on them.

Compared to performance analysis and optimization at a smaller component level, as we saw in previous chapters, it takes a holistic approach to improve performance at the application level. The higher-level concerns, such as serving a certain number of users in a day, or handling an identified quantum of load through a multi-layered system, requires us to think about how the components fit together and how the load is designed to flow through it. In this chapter, we will discuss such high-level concerns. Like the previous chapter, by and large this chapter applies to applications written in any JVM language, but with a focus on Clojure. In this chapter, we will discuss general performance techniques that apply to all layers of the code:

- Choosing libraries
- Logging
- Data sizing
- Resource pooling
- Fetch and compute in advance
- Staging and batching
- Little's law

Choosing libraries

Most non-trivial applications depend a great deal on third-party libraries for various functionality, such as logging, serving web requests, connecting to databases, writing to message queues, and so on. Many of these libraries not only carry out parts of critical business functionality but also appear in the performance-sensitive areas of our code, impacting the overall performance. It is imperative that we choose libraries wisely (with respect to features versus performance trade off) after due performance analysis.

The crucial factor in choosing libraries is not identifying which library to use, rather it is having a performance model of our applications and having the use cases benchmarked under representative load. Only benchmarks can tell us whether the performance is problematic or acceptable. If the performance is below expectation, a drill-down profiling can show us whether a third-party library is causing the performance issue. In *Chapter 6, Measuring Performance* and *Chapter 7, Performance Optimization* we discussed how to measure performance and identify bottlenecks. You can evaluate multiple libraries for performance-sensitive use cases and choose what suits.

Libraries often improve (or occasionally lose) performance with new releases, so measurement and profiling (comparative, across versions) should be an ongoing practice for the development and maintenance lifecycle of our applications. Another factor to note is that libraries may show different performance characteristics based on the use case, load, and the benchmark. The devil is in the benchmark details. Be sure that your benchmarks are as close as possible to the representative scenario for your application.

Making a choice via benchmarks

Let's take a brief look at a few general use cases where performance of third-party libraries are exposed via benchmarks.

Web servers

Web servers are typically subject to quite a bit of performance benchmarking due to their generic nature and scope. One such benchmark for Clojure web servers exists here:

```
https://github.com/ptaoussanis/clojure-web-server-benchmarks
```

Web servers are complex pieces of software and they may exhibit different characteristics under various conditions. As you will notice, the performance numbers vary based on keep-alive versus non-keep-alive modes and request volume—at the time of writing, Immutant-2 came out better in keep-alive mode but fared poorly in the non-keep-alive benchmark. In production, people often front their application servers with reverse proxy servers, for example Nginx or HAProxy, which make keep-alive connections to application servers.

Web routing libraries

There are several web routing libraries for Clojure, as listed here:

```
https://github.com/juxt/bidi#comparison-with-other-routing-libraries
```

The same document also shows a performance benchmark with **Compojure** as the baseline, in which (at the time of writing) Compojure turns out to be performing better than **Bidi**. However, another benchmark compares Compojure, **Clout** (the library that Compojure internally uses), and **CalfPath** routing here:

```
https://github.com/kumarshantanu/calfpath#development
```

In this benchmark, as of this writing, Clout performs better than Compojure, and CalfPath outperforms Clout. However, you should be aware of any caveats in the faster libraries.

Data serialization

There are several ways to serialize data in Clojure, for example EDN and Fressian. Nippy is another serialization library with benchmarks to demonstrate how well it performs over EDN and Fressian:

```
https://github.com/ptaoussanis/nippy#performance
```

We covered Nippy in *Chapter 2, Clojure Abstractions* to show how it uses transients to speed up its internal computations. Even within Nippy, there are several flavors of serialization that have different features/performance trade-offs.

JSON serialization

Parsing and generating JSON is a very common use case in RESTful services and web applications. The Clojure contrib library clojure/data.json (`https://github.com/clojure/data.json`) provides this functionality. However, many people have found out that the Cheshire library `https://github.com/dakrone/cheshire` performs much better than the former. The included benchmarks in Cheshire can be run using the following command:

```
lein with-profile dev,benchmark test
```

Cheshire internally uses the Jackson Java library `https://github.com/FasterXML/jackson`, which is known for its good performance.

JDBC

JDBC access is another very common use case among applications using relational databases. The Clojure contrib library `clojure/java.jdbc` `https://github.com/clojure/java.jdbc` provides a Clojure JDBC API. Asphalt `https://github.com/kumarshantanu/asphalt` is an alternative JDBC library where the comparative benchmarks can be run as follows:

```
lein with-profile dev,c17,perf test
```

As of this writing, Asphalt outperforms `clojure/java.jdbc` by several micro seconds, which may be useful in low-latency applications. However, note that JDBC performance is usually dominated by SQL queries/joins, database latency, connection pool parameters, and so on. We will discuss more about JDBC in later sections.

Logging

Logging is a prevalent activity that almost all non-trivial applications do. Logging calls are quite frequent, hence it is important to make sure our logging configuration is tuned well for performance. If you are not familiar with logging systems (especially on the JVM), you may want to take some time to get familiar with those first. We will cover the use of `clojure/tools.logging`, **SLF4J** and **LogBack** libraries (as a combination) for logging, and look into how to make them perform well:

- Clojure/tools.logging `https://github.com/clojure/tools.logging`
- SLF4J: `http://www.slf4j.org/`
- LogBack: `http://logback.qos.ch/`

Why SLF4J/LogBack?

Besides SLF4J/LogBack, there are several logging libraries to choose from in the Clojure application, for example Timbre, Log4j and java.util.logging. While there is nothing wrong with these libraries, we are often constrained into choosing something that covers most other third-party libraries (also including Java libraries) in our applications for logging purposes. SLF4J is a Java logger facade that detects any available implementation (LogBack, Log4j, and so on) — we choose LogBack simply because it performs well and is highly configurable. The library clojure/tools. logging provides a Clojure logging API that detects SLF4J, Log4j or java.util.logging (in that order) in the classpath and uses whichever implementation is found first.

The setup

Let's walk through how to set up a logging system for your application using LogBack, SLF4J and `clojure/tools.logging` for a project built using Leiningen.

Dependencies

Your `project.clj` file should have the LogBack, SLF4J and `clojure/tools. logging` dependencies under the `:dependencies` key:

```
[ch.qos.logback/logback-classic "1.1.2"]
[ch.qos.logback/logback-core    "1.1.2"]
[org.slf4j/slf4j-api            "1.7.9"]
[org.codehaus.janino/janino     "2.6.1"]  ; for Logback-config
[org.clojure/tools.logging      "0.3.1"]
```

The previously mentioned versions are current and work as of the time of writing. You may want to use updated versions, if available.

The logback configuration file

You need to create a `logback.xml` file in the `resources` directory:

```
<?xml version="1.0" encoding="UTF-8"?>
<configuration>

  <appender name="FILE"
            class="ch.qos.logback.core.rolling.RollingFileAppender">
    <file>${logfile.general.name:-logs/application.log}</file>
    <rollingPolicy class="ch.qos.logback.core.rolling.
TimeBasedRollingPolicy">
```

```
        <!-- daily rollover -->
        <fileNamePattern>${logfile.general.name:-logs/application.
log}.%d{yyyy-MM-dd}.%i.gz</fileNamePattern>
        <timeBasedFileNamingAndTriggeringPolicy class="ch.qos.logback.
core.rolling.SizeAndTimeBasedFNATP">
            <!-- or whenever the file size reaches 100MB -->
            <maxFileSize>100MB</maxFileSize>
        </timeBasedFileNamingAndTriggeringPolicy>
        <!-- keep 30 days worth of history -->
        <maxHistory>30</maxHistory>
    </rollingPolicy>
    <append>true</append>
    <encoder class="ch.qos.logback.core.encoder.
LayoutWrappingEncoder">
        <layout class="ch.qos.logback.classic.PatternLayout">
            <pattern%d{HH:mm:ss.SSS} [%thread] %-5level %logger{36} -
%msg%n</pattern>
        </layout>
        <immediateFlush>false</immediateFlush>
    </encoder>
  </appender>

  <appender name="AsyncFile" class="ch.qos.logback.classic.
AsyncAppender">
    <queueSize>500</queueSize>
    <discardingThreshold>0</discardingThreshold>
    <appender-ref ref="FILE" />
  </appender>

  <!-- You may want to set the level to DEBUG in development -->
  <root level="ERROR">
    <appender-ref ref="AsyncFile" />
  </root>

  <!-- Replace com.example with base namespace of your app -->
  <logger name="com.example" additivity="false">
    <!-- You may want to set the level to DEBUG in development -->
    <level value="INFO"/>
    <appender-ref ref="AsyncFile" />
  </logger>

</configuration>
```

The previous logback.xml file is simple on purpose (for illustration) and has just enough configuration to get you started with logging using LogBack.

Optimization

The optimization points are highlighted in the `logback.xml` file we saw earlier in this section. We set the `immediateFlush` attribute to `false` such that the messages are buffered before flushing to the appender. We also wrapped the regular file appender with an asynchronous appender and edited the `queueSize` and `discardingThreshold` attributes, which gets us much better results than the default.

Unless optimized, logging configurations are usually a common source of suboptimal performance in many applications. Usually, the performance problems show up only at high load when the log volume is very high. The optimizations discussed previously are only a few of the many possible optimizations that one can experiment with. The chapters in LogBack documentation, such as **encoders** (`http://logback.qos.ch/manual/encoders.html`), **appenders** (`http://logback.qos.ch/manual/appenders.html`) and **configuration** (`http://logback.qos.ch/manual/configuration.html`) have useful **information**. There are also tips `http://blog.takipi.com/how-to-instantly-improve-your-java-logging-with-7-logback-tweaks/` on the Internet that may provide useful pointers.

Data sizing

The cost of abstractions in terms of the data size plays an important role. For example, whether or not a data element can fit into a processor cache line depends directly upon its size. On a Linux system, we can find out the cache line size and other parameters by inspecting the values in the files under the `/sys/devices/system/cpu/cpu0/cache/` directory. Refer to *Chapter 4, Host Performance*, where we discussed how to compute the size of primitives, objects, and data elements.

Another concern we generally find with data sizing is how much data we hold at any time in the heap. As we noted in earlier chapters, GC has direct consequences on the application performance. While processing data, often we do not really need all the data we hold on to. Consider the example of generating a summary report of sold items for a certain period (months) of time. After the subperiod (month-wise) summary data is computed, we do not need the item details anymore, hence it's better to remove the unwanted data while we add the summaries. See the following example:

```
(defn summarize [daily-data]  ; daily-data is a map
  (let [s (items-summary (:items daily-data))]
    (-> daily-data
      (select-keys [:digest :invoices])  ; keep required k/v pairs
```

```
        (assoc :summary s))))

;; now inside report generation code
(-> (fetch-items period-from period-to :interval-day)
  (map summarize)
  generate-report)
```

Had we not used `select-keys` in the previous `summarize` function, it would have returned a map with extra `:summary` data along with all other existing keys in the map. Now, such a thing is often combined with lazy sequences, so for this scheme to work it is important not to hold onto the head of the lazy sequence. Recall that in *Chapter 2, Clojure Abstractions* we discussed the perils of holding onto the head of a lazy sequence.

Reduced serialization

We discussed in earlier chapters that serialization over an I/O channel is a common source of latency. The perils of over-serialization cannot be overstated. Whether we read or write data from a data source over an I/O channel, all of that data needs to be prepared, encoded, serialized, de-serialized, and parsed before being worked upon. The less data that is involved, the better it is for every step in order to lower the overhead. Where there is no I/O involved (such as in-process communication), it generally makes no sense to serialize.

A common example of over-serialization is when working with SQL databases. Often, there are common SQL query functions that fetch all columns of a table or a relation—they are called by various functions that implement business logic. Fetching data that we do not need is wasteful and detrimental to performance for the same reason that we discussed in the previous paragraph. While it may seem more work to write one SQL statement and one database-query function for each use case, it pays off with better performance. Code that uses NoSQL databases is also subject to this anti-pattern—we have to take care to fetch only what we need even though it may lead to additional code.

There's a pitfall to be aware of when reducing serialization. Often, some information needs to be inferred in the absence of serialized data. In such cases, where some of the serialization is dropped so that we can infer other information, we must compare the cost of inference versus the serialization overhead. The comparison may not necessarily be only per operation, but rather on the whole, such that we can consider the resources we can allocate in order to achieve capacities for various parts of our systems.

Chunking to reduce memory pressure

What happens when we slurp a text file regardless of its size? The contents of the entire file will sit in the JVM heap. If the file is larger than the JVM heap capacity, the JVM will terminate, throwing OutOfMemoryError. If the file is large, but not enough to force the JVM into OOM error, it leaves relatively less JVM heap space for other operations to continue in the application. Similar situations take place when we carry out any operation disregarding the JVM heap capacity. Fortunately, this can be fixed by reading data in chunks and processing them before reading more. In *Chapter 3*, *Leaning on Java*, we briefly discussed memory mapped buffers, which is another complementary solution that you may like to explore.

Sizing for file/network operations

Let's take the example of a data ingestion process where a semi-automated job uploads large **Comma Separated File (CSV)** files via **File Transfer Protocol (FTP)** to a file server, and another automated job (written in Clojure) runs periodically to detect the arrival of files via a Network File System (NFS). After detecting a new file, the Clojure program processes the file, updates the result in a database, and archives the file. The program detects and processes several files concurrently. The size of the CSV files is not known in advance, but the format is predefined.

As per the previous description, one potential problem is, since there could be multiple files being processed concurrently, how do we distribute the JVM heap among the concurrent file-processing jobs? Another issue at hand could be that the operating system imposes a limit on how many files could be open at a time; on Unix-like systems you can use the ulimit command to extend the limit. We cannot arbitrarily slurp the CSV file contents—we must limit each job to a certain amount of memory, and also limit the number of jobs that can run concurrently. At the same time, we cannot read a very small number of rows from a file at a time because this may impact performance:

```
(def ^:const K 1024)

;; create the buffered reader using custom 128K buffer-size
(-> filename
  java.io.FileInputStream.
  java.io.InputStreamReader.
  (java.io.BufferedReader. (* K 128)))
```

Fortunately, we can specify the buffer size when reading from a file (or even from a network stream) so as to tune the memory usage and performance as appropriate. In the previous code example, we explicitly set the buffer size of the reader to facilitate the same.

Sizing for JDBC query results

Java's interface standard for SQL databases, JDBC (which is technically not an acronym), supports *fetch size* for fetching query results via JDBC drivers. The default fetch size depends on the JDBC driver. Most of the JDBC drivers keep a low default value to avoid high memory usage and for internal performance optimization reasons. A notable exception to this norm is the MySQL JDBC driver that completely fetches and stores all rows in memory by default:

```clojure
(require '[clojure.java.jdbc :as jdbc])


;; using prepare-statement directly
(with-open
  [stmt (jdbc/prepare-statement
          conn sql :fetch-size 1000 :max-rows 9000)
   rset (resultset-seq (.executeQuery stmt))]
  (vec rset))


;; using query
(jdbc/query db [{:fetch-size 1000}
          "SELECT empno FROM emp WHERE country=?" 1])
```

When using the Clojure contrib library `java.jdbc` (`https://github.com/clojure/java.jdbc` as of version 0.3.7), the fetch size can be set while preparing a statement as shown in the previous example. Note that the fetch size does not guarantee proportional latency; however, it can be used safely for memory sizing. We must test any performance-impacting latency changes due to fetch size at different loads and use cases for the particular database and JDBC driver. Another important factor to note is that the benefit of `:fetch-size` can be useful only if the query result set is consumed incrementally and lazily — if a function extracts all rows from a result set to create a vector, then the benefit of `:fetch-size` is nullified from a memory conservation point of view. Besides fetch size, we can also pass the `:max-rows` argument to limit the maximum rows to be returned by a query — however, this implies that the extra rows will be truncated from the result, and not whether the database will internally limit the number of rows to realize.

Resource pooling

There are several types of resources on the JVM that are rather expensive to initialize. Examples are HTTP connections, execution threads, JDBC connections, and so on. The Java API recognizes such resources and has built-in support for creating a pool of some of those resources, such that the consumer code borrows a resource from a pool when required and at the end of the job simply returns it to the pool. Java's thread pools (discussed in *Chapter 5, Concurrency*) and JDBC data sources are prominent examples. The idea is to preserve the initialized objects for reuse. Even though Java does not support pooling of a resource type directly, one can always create a pool abstraction around custom expensive resources. Note that the pooling technique is common in I/O activities, but can be equally applicable to non-I/O purposes where initialization cost is high.

JDBC resource pooling

Java supports the obtaining of JDBC connections via the `javax.sql.DataSource` interface, which can be pooled. A JDBC connection pool implements this interface. Typically, a JDBC connection pool is implemented by third-party libraries or a JDBC driver itself. Generally, very few JDBC drivers implement a connection pool, so Open Source third-party JDBC resource pooling libraries such as Apache DBCP, c3p0, BoneCP, HikariCP, and so on are popular. They also support validation queries for eviction of stale connections that might result from network timeouts and firewalls, and guard against connection leaks. Apache DBCP and HikariCP are accessible from Clojure via their respective Clojure wrapper libraries Clj-DBCP (`https://github.com/kumarshantanu/clj-dbcp`) and HikariCP (`https://github.com/tomekw/hikari-cp`), and there are Clojure examples describing how to construct C3P0 and BoneCP pools (`http://clojure-doc.org/articles/ecosystem/java_jdbc/connection_pooling.html`).

Connections are not the only JDBC resources that need to be pooled. Every time we create a new JDBC prepared statement, depending on the JDBC driver implementation, often the entire statement template is sent to the database server in order to obtain a reference to the prepared statement. As the database servers are generally deployed on separate hardware, there may be network latency involved. Hence, the pooling of prepared statements is a very desirable property of JDBC resource pooling libraries. Apache DBCP, C3P0, and BoneCP all support statement pooling, and the Clj-DBCP wrapper enables the pooling of prepared statements out-of-the-box for better performance. HikariCP has the opinion that statement pooling, nowadays, is already done internally by JDBC drivers, hence explicit pooling is not required. I would strongly advise running your benchmarks with the connection pooling libraries to determine whether or not it really works for your JDBC driver and application.

I/O batching and throttling

It is well known that chatty I/O calls generally lead to poor performance. In general, the solution is to batch together several messages and send them in one payload. In databases and network calls, batching is a common and useful technique to improve throughput. On the other hand, large batch sizes may actually harm throughput as they tend to incur memory overhead, and components may not be ready to handle a large batch at once. Hence, sizing the batches and throttling are just as important as batching. I would strongly advise conducting your own tests to determine the optimum batch size under representative load.

JDBC batch operations

JDBC has long had batch-update support in its API, which includes the INSERT, UPDATE, DELETE statements. The Clojure contrib library java.jdbc supports JDBC batch operations via its own API, as we can see as follows:

```
(require '[clojure.java.jdbc :as jdbc])

;; multiple SQL statements
(jdbc/db-do-commands
  db true
  ["INSERT INTO emp (name, countrycode) VALUES ('John Smith', 3)"
   "UPDATE emp SET countrycode=4 WHERE empid=1379"])

;; similar statements with only different parametrs
(jdbc/db-do-prepared
  db true
  "UPDATE emp SET countrycode=? WHERE empid=?"
  [4 1642]
  [9 1186]
  [2 1437])
```

Besides batch-update support, we can also batch JDBC queries. One of the common techniques is to use the SQL WHERE clause to avoid the N+1 selects issue. The N+1 issue indicates the situation when we execute one query in another child table for every row in a rowset from a master table. A similar technique can be used to combine several similar queries on the same table into just one, and segregate the data in the program afterwards.

Consider the following example that uses clojure.java.jdbc 0.3.7 and the MySQL database:

```
(require '[clojure.java.jdbc :as j])

(def db {:subprotocol "mysql"
         :subname "//127.0.0.1:3306/clojure_test"
         :user "clojure_test" :password "clojure_test"})

;; the snippet below uses N+1 selects
;; (typically characterized by SELECT in a loop)
(def rq "select order_id from orders where status=?")
(def tq "select * from items where fk_order_id=?")
(doseq [order (j/query db [rq "pending"])]
  (let [items (j/query db [tq (:order_id order)])]
    ;; do something with items
    ...))

;; the snippet below avoids N+1 selects,
;; but requires fk_order_id to be indexed
(def jq "select t.* from orders r, items t
  where t.fk_order_id=r.order_id and r.status=? order by t.fk_order_
id")
(let [all-items (group-by :fk_order_id (j/query db [jq "pending"]))]
  (doseq [[order-id items] all-items]
    ;; do something with items
    ...))
```

In the previous example there are two tables: orders and items. The first snippet reads all order IDs from the orders table, and then iterates through them to query corresponding entries in the items table in a loop. This is the N+1 selects performance anti-pattern you should keep an eye on. The second snippet avoids N+1 selects by issuing a single SQL query, but may not perform very well unless the column fk_order_id is indexed.

Batch support at API level

When designing any service, it is very useful to provide an API for batch operations. This builds flexibility in the API such that batch sizing and throttling can be controlled in a fine-grained manner. Not surprisingly, it is also an effective recipe for building high-performance services. A common overhead we encounter when implementing batch operations is the identification of each item in the batch and their correlation across requests and responses. The problem becomes more prominent when requests are asynchronous.

The solution to the item identification issue is resolved either by assigning a canonical or global ID to each item in the request (batch), or by assigning every request (batch) a unique ID and each item in the request an ID that is local to the batch.

The choice of the exact solution usually depends on the implementation details. When requests are synchronous, you can do away with identification of each request item (see the Facebook API for reference: `http://developers.facebook.com/docs/reference/api/batch/`) where the items in response follow the same order as in the request. However, in asynchronous requests, items may have to be tracked via status-check call or callbacks. The desired tracking granularity typically guides the appropriate item identification strategy.

For example, if we have a batch API for order processing, every order would have a unique Order-ID that can be used in subsequent status-check calls. In another example, let's say there is a batch API for creating API keys for **Internet of Things (IoT)** devices — here, the API keys are not known beforehand, but they can be generated and returned in a synchronous response. However, if this has to be an asynchronous batch API, the service should respond with a batch request ID that can be used later to find the status of the request. In a batch response for the request ID, the server can include request item IDs (for example device IDs, which may be unique for the client but not unique across all clients) with their respective status.

Throttling requests to services

As every service can handle only a certain capacity, the rate at which we send requests to a service is important. The expectations about the service behavior are generally in terms of both throughput and latency. This requires us to send requests at a specified rate, as a rate lower than that may lead to under-utilization of the service, and a higher rate may overload the service or result in failure, thus leading to client-side under-utilization.

Let's say a third-party service can accept 100 requests per second. However, we may not know how robustly the service is implemented. Though sometimes it is not exactly specified, sending 100 requests at once (within 20ms, let's say) during each second may lead to lower throughput than expected. Evenly distributing the requests across the one-second duration, for example sending one request every 10ms (1000ms / 100 = 10ms), may increase the chance of attaining the optimum throughput.

For throttling, **Token bucket** (`https://en.wikipedia.org/wiki/Token_bucket`) and **Leaky bucket** (`https://en.wikipedia.org/wiki/Leaky_bucket`) algorithms can be useful. Throttling at a very fine-grained level requires that we buffer the items so that we can maintain a uniform rate. Buffering consumes memory and often requires ordering; queues (covered in *Chapter 5, Concurrency*), pipeline and persistent storage usually serve that purpose well. Again, buffering and queuing may be subject to back pressure due to system constraints. We will discuss pipelines, back pressure and buffering in a later section in this chapter.

Precomputing and caching

While processing data, we usually come across instances where few common computation steps precede several kinds of subsequent steps. That is to say, some amount of computation is common and the remaining is different. For high-latency common computations (I/O to access the data and memory/CPU to process it), it makes a lot of sense to compute them once and store in digest form, such that the subsequent steps can simply use the digest data and proceed from that point onward, thus resulting in reduced overall latency. This is also known as staging of semi-computed data and is a common technique to optimize processing of non-trivial data.

Clojure has decent support for caching. The built-in `clojure.core/memoize` function performs basic caching of computed results with no flexibility in using specific caching strategies and pluggable backends. The Clojure contrib library `core.memoize` offsets the lack of flexibility in `memoize` by providing several configuration options. Interestingly, the features in `core.memoize` are also useful as a separate caching library, so the common portion is factored out as a Clojure contrib library called `core.cache` on top of which `core.memoize` is implemented.

As many applications are deployed on multiple servers for availability, scaling and maintenance reasons, they need distributed caching that is fast and space efficient. The open source memcached project is a popular in-memory, distributed key-value/object store that can act as a caching server for web applications. It hashes the keys to identify the server to store the value on, and has no out-of-the-box replication or persistence. It is used to cache database query results, computation results, and so on. For Clojure, there is a memcached client library called SpyGlass (`https://github.com/clojurewerkz/spyglass`). Of course, memcached is not limited to just web applications; it can be used for other purposes too.

Concurrent pipelines

Imagine a situation where we have to carry out jobs at a certain throughput, such that each job includes the same sequence of differently sized I/O task (task A), a memory-bound task (task B) and, again, an I/O task (task C). A naïve approach would be to create a thread pool and run each job off it, but soon we realize that this is not optimum because we cannot ascertain the utilization of each I/O resource due to unpredictability of the threads being scheduled by the OS. We also observe that even though several concurrent jobs have similar I/O tasks, we are unable to batch them in our first approach.

As the next iteration, we split each job in stages (A, B, C), such that each stage corresponds to one task. Since the tasks are well known, we create one thread pool (of appropriate size) per stage and execute tasks in them. The result of task A is required by task B, and B's result is required by task C — we enable this communication via queues. Now, we can tune the thread pool size for each stage, batch the I/O tasks, and throttle them for an optimum throughput. This kind of an arrangement is a concurrent pipeline. Some readers may find this feebly resembling the actor model or **Staged Event Driven Architecture (SEDA)** model, which are more refined models for this kind of approach. Recall that we discussed several kinds of in-process queues in *Chapter 5, Concurrency*.

Distributed pipelines

With this approach, it is possible to scale out the job execution to multiple hosts in a cluster using network queues, thereby offloading memory consumption, durability, and delivery to the queue infrastructure. For example, in a given scenario there could be several nodes in a cluster, all of them running the same code and exchanging messages (requests and intermediate result data) via network queues.

The following diagram depicts how a simple invoice-generation system might be connected to network queues:

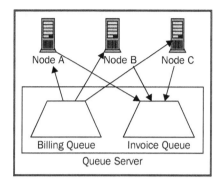

RabbitMQ, HornetQ, ActiveMQ, Kestrel and Kafka are some well-known Open Source queue systems. Once in a while, the jobs may require distributed state and coordination. The Avout (`http://avout.io/`) project implements the distributed version of Clojure's atom and ref, which can be used for this purpose. Tesser (`https://github.com/aphyr/tesser`) is another library for local and distributed parallelism using Clojure. The Storm (`http://storm-project.net/`) and Onyx (`http://www.onyxplatform.org/`) projects are distributed, real-time stream processing systems implemented using Clojure.

Applying back pressure

We discussed back pressure briefly in the last chapter. Without back pressure we cannot build a reasonable load-tolerant system with predictable stability and performance. In this section, we will see how to apply back pressure in different scenarios in an application. At a fundamental level, we should have a threshold of a maximum number of concurrent jobs in the system and, based on that threshold, we should reject new requests above a certain arrival rate. The rejected messages may either be retried by the client or ignored if there is no control over the client. When applying back pressure to user-facing services, it may be useful to detect system load and deny auxiliary services first in order to conserve capacity and degrade gracefully in the face of high load.

Thread pool queues

JVM thread pools are backed by queues, which means that when we submit
a job into a thread pool that already has the maximum jobs running, the new job
lands in the queue. The queue is by default an unbounded queue, which is not
suitable for applying back pressure. So, we have to create the thread pool backed
by a bounded queue:

```
(import 'java.util.concurrent.LinkedBlockingDeque)
(import 'java.util.concurrent.TimeUnit)
(import 'java.util.concurrent.ThreadPoolExecutor)
(import 'java.util.concurrent.ThreadPoolExecutor$AbortPolicy)
(def tpool
  (let [q (LinkedBlockingDeque. 100)
        p (ThreadPoolExecutor$AbortPolicy.)]
    (ThreadPoolExecutor. 1 10 30 TimeUnit/SECONDS q p)))
```

Now, on this pool, whenever there is an attempt to add more jobs than the
capacity of the queue, it will throw an exception. The caller should treat the
exception as a buffer-full condition and wait until the buffer has idle capacity
again by periodically pooling the java.util.concurrent.BlockingQueue.
remainingCapacity() method.

Servlet containers such as Tomcat and Jetty

In the synchronous **Tomcat** and **Jetty** versions, each HTTP request is given a
dedicated thread from a common thread pool that a user can configure. The number
of simultaneous requests being served is limited by the thread pool size. A common
way to control the arrival rate is to set the thread pool size of the server. The
Ring library uses an embedded jetty server by default in development mode.
The embedded Jetty adapter (in Ring) can be programmatically configured
with a thread pool size.

In the asynchronous (Async Servlet 3.0) versions of Tomcat and Jetty beside the
thread pool size, it is also possible to specify the timeout for processing each request.
However, note that the thread pool size does not limit the number of requests in
asynchronous versions in the way it does on synchronous versions. The request
processing is transferred to an ExecutorService (thread pool), which may buffer
requests until a thread is available. This buffering behavior is tricky because this may
cause system overload — you can override the default behavior by defining your own
thread pool instead of using the servlet container's thread pool to return a HTTP
error at a certain threshold of waiting requests.

HTTP Kit

HTTP Kit (http://http-kit.org/) is a high-performance asynchronous (based on Java NIO implementation) web server for Clojure. It has built-in support for applying back pressure to new requests via a specified queue length. As of HTTP Kit 2.1.19, see the following snippet:

```
(require '[org.httpkit.server :as hk])

;; handler is a typical Ring handler
(hk/run-server handler {:port 3000 :thread 32 :queue-size 600})
```

In the previous snippet, the worker thread pool size is 32 and the max queue length is specified as 600. When not specified, 20480 is the default maximum queue length for applying back pressure.

Aleph

Aleph (http://aleph.io/) is another high-performance asynchronous web server based on the Java Netty (http://netty.io/) library, which in turn is based on Java NIO. Aleph extends Netty with its own primitives compatible with Netty. The worker thread pool in Aleph is specified via an option, as we can see in the following snippet as of Aleph 0.4.0:

```
(require '[aleph.http :as a])

;; handler is a typical Ring handler
(a/start-server handler {:executor tpool})
```

Here, tpool refers to a bounded thread pool as discussed in the subsection *Thread pool queues*. By default, Aleph uses a dynamic thread pool capped at maximum 512 threads aimed at 90 percent system utilization via the **Dirigiste** (https://github. com/ztellman/dirigiste) library.

Back pressure not only involves enqueuing a limited number of jobs, but slows down the processing rate of a job when the peer is slow. Aleph deals with per-request back pressure (for example, when streaming response data) by "not accepting data until it runs out of memory" — it falls back to blocking instead of dropping data, or raising exceptions and closing connections

Performance and queueing theory

If we observe the performance benchmark numbers across a number of runs, even though the hardware, loads and OS remain the same, the numbers are rarely exactly the same. The difference between each run may be as much as -8 percent to 8 percent for no apparent reason. This may seem surprising, but the deep-rooted reason is that the performances of computer systems are *stochastic* by nature. There are many small factors in a computer system that make performance unpredictable at any given point of time. At best, the performance variations can be explained by a series of probabilities over random variables.

The basic premise is that each subsystem is more or less like a queue where requests await their turn to be served. The CPU has an instruction queue with unpredictable fetch/decode/branch-predict timings, the memory access again depends on cache hit ratio and whether it needs to be dispatched via the interconnect, and the I/O subsystem works using interrupts that may again depend on mechanical factors of the I/O device. The OS schedules threads that wait while not executing. The software built on the top of all this basically waits in various queues to get the job done.

Little's law

Little's law states that, over steady state, the following holds true:

$$mean\ number\ of\ jobs\ in\ a\ system = mean\ arrival\ rate \times mean\ response\ time$$

$$mean\ number\ of\ jobs\ in\ the\ queue = mean\ arrival\ rate \times mean\ waiting\ time$$

This is a rather important law that gives us insight into the system capacity as it is independent of other factors. For an example, if the average time to satisfy a request is 200 ms and the service rate is about 70 per second, then the mean number of requests being served is *70 req/second x 0.2 second = 14 requests.*

Note that Little's law does not talk about spikes in request arrival rate or spikes in latency (due to GC and/or other bottlenecks) or system behavior in response to these factors. When the arrival rate spikes at one point, your system must have enough resources to handle the number of concurrent tasks required to serve the requests. We can infer here that Little's law is helpful to measure and tune average system behavior over a duration, but we cannot plan capacity based solely on this.

Performance tuning with respect to Little's law

In order to maintain good throughput, we should strive to maintain an upper limit on the total number of tasks in the system. Since there can be many kinds of tasks in a system and lot of tasks can happily co-exist in the absence of bottlenecks, a better way to say it is to ensure that the system utilization and bottlenecks remain in limit.

Often, the arrival rate may not be within the control of a system. For such scenarios, the only option is to minimize the latency as much as possible and deny new requests after a certain threshold of total jobs in the system. You may be able to know the right threshold only through performance and load tests. If you can control the arrival rate, you can throttle the arrival (based on performance and load tests) so as to maintain a steady flow.

Summary

Designing an application for performance should be based on the use cases and patterns of anticipated system load and behavior. Measuring performance is extremely important to guide optimization in the process. Fortunately, there are several well-known optimization patterns to tap into, such as resource pooling, data sizing, pre-fetch and pre-compute, staging, batching, and so on. As it turns out, application performance is not only a function of the use cases and patterns — the system as a whole is a continuous stochastic turn of events that can be assessed statistically and is guided by probability. Clojure is a fun language to do high-performance programming. This book prescribes many pointers and practices for performance, but there is no mantra that can solve everything. The devil is in the details. Know the idioms and patterns, experiment to see what works for your applications, and know which rules you can bend for performance.

Index

Symbols

.class files
  decompiling, into Java source 36, 37

A

Abstract Syntax Tree (AST) 44
Aleph
  URL 161
Amdahl's Law 96
amortization 22
AppDynamics
  URL 138
array
  about 40, 41
  using, for efficiency 46
array of primitives 43
Asphalt
  URL 146
assertions
  disabling, in production 29, 30
  reference link 29
Asynchronous Agents
  about 76, 77
  state 76, 77
  using 79
asynchrony 78
atomic updates
  about 72
  and state 72
  faster writes, with atom striping 75, 76
  in Java 73
  support, Clojure 74-76
autopromotion 39

Avout
  URL 159

B

back pressure, applying
  about 159
  Aleph 161
  HTTP Kit 161
  Jetty 160
  thread pool queues 160
  Tomcat 160
bandwidth 7, 8
baseline 8
batch processing 5
benchmark 8
Big-O notation 20
boxed math
  detecting 50
boxed numerics 38
boxplot 104
branch prediction 54
bubbles 54
bytebuffer
  URL 65

C

cache 56, 57
cache bound task 3
cachegrind
  URL 64
cache-oblivious algorithms 3
caching 157

protocols

  versus multimethods 32

proxy-super macro 46

Q

queueing 78, 162

QuickPath 57

R

recursion 30

reducing function 26

reference types

  validating 87, 88

  watching 87, 88

reflection 42

Relaxed Radix Balanced (RRB) 20

Relic

  URL 138

REPL 38

requests

  throttling, to services 156

resource pooling

  about 153

  JDBC resource pooling 153

resource utilization 10

Riemann

  URL 116

Ring

  reference link 117

Ring-based

  URL 129

Ring library 160

RRB-trees paper

  references 20

S

Sampler tab 135

  about 135

  thread name, setting 135, 136

sampling profilers 9

sequences

  about 21

  first function 21

  next function 21

  rest function 21

services

  requests, throttling to 156

setup, logging

  about 147

  dependencies 147

  logback configuration file 147, 148

  optimization 149

Simultaneous multithreading (SMT) 55

SLF4J

  about 146

  need for 147

  URL 146

SpyGlass

  URL 157

Staged Event Driven Architecture
    (SEDA) 158

stalls 54

standard deviation 106

static instruction scheduling 54

statistics terminology primer

  about 104

  boxplot 104

  first quartile 104

  frequency 105

  mean 104

  median 104

  percentile 105

  periods 105

  standard deviation 106

  third quartile 104

  variance 106

Statsd 116

StatsD

  URL 116

storage 57

Storm

  URL 159

stress testing 115

string concatenation 45

Stringer

  URL 45

string interning 14

strings 14

structured approach, to performance 5, 6

symbols 15

Symmetric multiprocessing (SMP) 57

T

tail-call optimization (TCO) 30
Tesser
  URL 159
third quartile 104
threads 55
Threads tab
  about 134, 135
  monitor state 135
  park state 135
  running state 134
  sleeping state 134
  wait state 134
throttling 154
throughput 7
throughput, performance testing
  average throughput test 112-115
  measuring 112
Token Bucket
  URL 157
Tomcat 160
transducer
  about 26, 27
  performance characteristics 27
transients
  about 28
  fast repetition 29
type hints 42

U

Universal Scalability Law 97
use case classification
  about 2
  batch processing 5
  computational and data-processing tasks 2
  online analytical processing (OLAP) 4
  online transaction processing (OLTP) 4
  user-facing software 2
user-facing software 2
USL
  URL 97

V

value 15
variable 16
variance 106
Visual GC tab 137
VisualVM
  URL 132
  used, for profiling code 132
vnStat tool 121

W

web-routing libraries 145
web server 144
workload 10
write absorption 69
write-buffer 69
write skew
  URL 83

Y

YourKit
  URL 138

Thank you for buying
Clojure High Performance Programming
Second Edition

About Packt Publishing

Packt, pronounced 'packed', published its first book, *Mastering phpMyAdmin for Effective MySQL Management*, in April 2004, and subsequently continued to specialize in publishing highly focused books on specific technologies and solutions.

Our books and publications share the experiences of your fellow IT professionals in adapting and customizing today's systems, applications, and frameworks. Our solution-based books give you the knowledge and power to customize the software and technologies you're using to get the job done. Packt books are more specific and less general than the IT books you have seen in the past. Our unique business model allows us to bring you more focused information, giving you more of what you need to know, and less of what you don't.

Packt is a modern yet unique publishing company that focuses on producing quality, cutting-edge books for communities of developers, administrators, and newbies alike. For more information, please visit our website at www.packtpub.com.

About Packt Open Source

In 2010, Packt launched two new brands, Packt Open Source and Packt Enterprise, in order to continue its focus on specialization. This book is part of the Packt Open Source brand, home to books published on software built around open source licenses, and offering information to anybody from advanced developers to budding web designers. The Open Source brand also runs Packt's Open Source Royalty Scheme, by which Packt gives a royalty to each open source project about whose software a book is sold.

Writing for Packt

We welcome all inquiries from people who are interested in authoring. Book proposals should be sent to author@packtpub.com. If your book idea is still at an early stage and you would like to discuss it first before writing a formal book proposal, then please contact us; one of our commissioning editors will get in touch with you.

We're not just looking for published authors; if you have strong technical skills but no writing experience, our experienced editors can help you develop a writing career, or simply get some additional reward for your expertise.

Clojure High Performance Programming

ISBN: 978-1-78216-560-6   Paperback: 152 pages

Understand performance aspects and write high performance code with Clojure

1. See how the hardware and the JVM impact performance.

2. Learn which Java features to use with Clojure, and how.

3. Deep dive into Clojure's concurrency and state primitives.

4. Discover how to design Clojure programs for performance.

Clojure Reactive Programming

ISBN: 978-1-78398-666-8   Paperback: 232 pages

Design and implement highly reusable reactive applications by integrating different frameworks with Clojure

1. Learn how to leverage the features of functional reactive programming using Clojure.

2. Create dataflow-based systems that are the building blocks of reactive programming.

3. Learn different Functional Reactive Programming frameworks and techniques by implementing real-world examples.

Please check **www.PacktPub.com** for information on our titles